D0372054

SELLEBRITY

SELLEBRITY

How to Build a Successful Sports & Entertainment Based Business

KOFI N. NARTEY, MBA

Sellebrity: How to Build a Successful Sports & Entertainment Based Business

Published by Grad Street Press
Marina del Rey, CA

Library of Congress Control Number: 2017937218
Nartey, Kofi N., Author

ISBN: 978-0-692-86384-8

BUSINESS & ECONOMICS / Sales & Selling

QUANTITY PURCHASES: Schools, companies, professional groups, clubs, and other organizations may qualify for special terms when ordering quantities of this title. For information, email info@GradStreetPress.

TO REALIZING POTENTIAL

Table of Contents

Acknowledgments

Thank you:

My writing & editing team: Robin Colucci, Bobby Haas, and Polly Letofsky.

My business friends and colleagues: Diane Hartley, Robert Reffkin, Bill Pipes, Laurie Moore-Moore, Lauren Beale, Lamin Turay, Dirk Rients, Peter Stougaard, Melissa McAvoy, Compass, and The Nartey Group agents and administrative team.

My friends and family, my parents, my kids Liya and Lincoln, and my amazing wife, Mimi.

&

God

SELLEBRITY NETWORK

THE SPORTS & ENTERTAINMENT SOCIETY

(www.TheSESociety.com)

Celebrity Real Estate & Luxury Lifestyle

With a desire and need to unite the sports and entertainment service providers nationally and globally, I created the "Sports & Entertainment Society."

The Sports & Entertainment Society is a group of real estate professionals, luxury lifestyle service providers, and companies that cater to sports and entertainment clientele. The Society offers membership opportunities for networking and referral business, marketing goods and services, ongoing training, best practices, and luxury lifestyle content.

The Society also offers consulting, certification and coaching programs.

Visit: www.TheSESociety.com

Introduction

Answering the Call

My work cell phone rang at 4:00 a.m. (which happens to be 6:00 a.m. in Chicago). Normally, I wouldn't answer it that early, but I happened to be up, and out of pure curiosity, I picked up the phone, "Hello?"

"Hello, Kofi?"

"Yes."

"How's it going? This is Michael Jordan."

"Get out of here."

"OK," Jordan chuckled.

I chuckled back. "I recognize that laugh. How's it going?"

"Good, good. I wanted to give you a call to talk about my house."

I was excited to know he had selected me to sell his highly celebrated Chicago home. We got into a conversation about the house, his motivations for building it, what he enjoyed about it, and my plan for selling it. We wrapped up with a side conversation on goal setting, focus, and achieving what you want in life. Glad I answered that 4:00 a.m. call.

Getting calls like that is what I dreamed of when I started to focus my real estate business in the sports and entertainment niche, but I wasn't quite sure how I would get those kinds of clients.

When I first entered real estate, I realized it was such a saturated industry that I had to distinguish myself with a specialty. At first, I focused on condos and townhomes because I owned a townhome at the time. It was going well, but I knew I could do more.

After a few years, I decided to focus on sports and entertainment. I had a handful of friends in the sports and entertainment industries and realized that it was a niche that required special understanding and care. As I got better at my craft, I knew I could carve out a niche servicing the real estate needs of sports and entertainment professionals. Many of my celebrity and affluent friends had been burned in business transactions or had received mediocre service. I wanted to specialize so that I could understand and meet their specific needs and elevate the level of service they received.

I sensed I had a better understanding and ability than others in my industry to service the sports and entertainment niche because I had played sports and worked as an actor for almost a decade before beginning my career in real estate. I identified the unique needs of sports and entertainment celebrities (and their business managers). I focused on the key things that made these transactions different from regular transactions in my industry.

This book is the culmination of that work. I have identified the best steps to move you towards a successful practice, and I offer you the insights and knowledge I have gained in building a sports and entertainment practice from scratch. While I had some unique advantages for breaking into this niche, everything I share in this book is transferable. I share my stories as examples to help expedite your learning and success. You can use these same tools and practices to avoid many of the pitfalls I encountered and create your own thriving business.

Today, I manage the largest sports and entertainment real estate team in the country, with over $1 billion of real estate under management.

Whether you are a Realtor®, attorney, financial advisor, business coach, personal trainer, insurance rep, or any other professional service provider, if you want to break into selling to and serving the sports and entertainment niche, this book is for you.

By reading this book, you will learn which unique qualities you possess that you can apply to your business so that you can get a head start on your competition and create a business that generates high-level leads and income in the world of sports and entertainment.

Both companies and individual service providers are realizing the need for a way to serve this special group. Businesses that kick off a sports and entertainment division today will have an advantage in the years to come. This book will help you do and say the right things to make it a success.

In today's market, it's not enough just to be a high-end or luxury business. The affluent consumer is buying a customized experience based on their personal preferences. Companies that are winning are those that are constantly learning about their clients and anticipating their needs. This is also true in the world of sports and entertainment celebrities, and it's up to you to market your goods and services in a way that appeals to them. You must demonstrate that you understand and can meet their lifestyle needs.

Let this book be your first mentor on this new venture. Use it as part of your journey of self-discovery as you uncover how you will effectively and successfully break into the sports and entertainment niche.

The best way to use this book is to read it all the way through once, then go back and read it again, working through each section.

Businesses that kick off a sports and entertainment division today will have an advantage in the years to come.

As you get into it, you'll notice I have sprinkled in several "Focus & Finish" tips. Focus and Finish has been my success mantra for the past several years. As an entrepreneur, I realized that the key to closing the gap between my ideas and my success was my ability to focus on and finish the steps to get there. It took focus and finish to create a successful luxury real estate practice that serves the entertainment and sports niche. I had to focus on developing the skills and tools to service this niche properly. Then, I had to systematize those tools and clarify my value proposition.

I used focus and finish to complete this book. I focused on it in between my real estate deals. I added to it after ongoing conversations with other successful, sports and entertainment-based professionals in other industries. I finished it after hours of sorting out the most effective ideas and strategies to pass along to you.

You will need to focus and finish to reach your goals. It will take focus for you to create a successful sports and entertainment based practice. You will have to finish the legwork. Finish the sales conversation. Finish the project so that your celebrity client is happy and satisfied.

Listen with Selfish Ears

Before I teach a seminar, I advise the audience to take a moment before we start and think about what they hope to get out of the class. I instruct them to think about their business model and the market for their business, and to listen for the ideas, techniques, and tools that could be most effective for them. In this book, I will share personal examples of what has worked for me (and what has failed miserably), and I will provide tools and duplicable techniques that you can use as a framework to create your own action steps. Read it with YOUR industry and YOUR goals in mind. If you do, you will be more open to the ideas, and your brain will create spaces for the most applicable ideas to land.

By the time you have finished the book, you can have your personal blueprint towards a successful sports and entertainment business.

Now, let's get started!

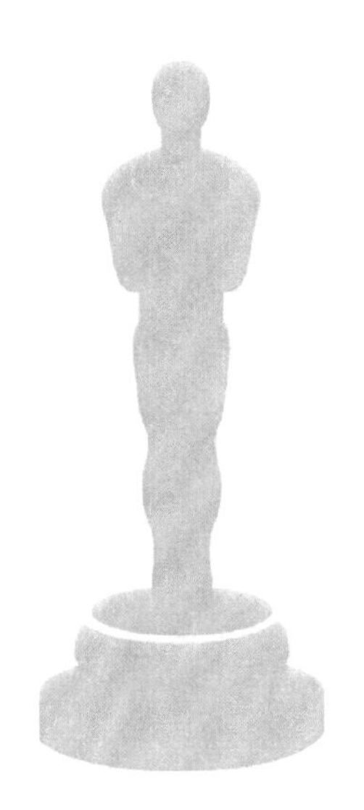

PART ONE

Getting Started

Getting Started

The Allure of Sports & Entertainment

Most people who want to break into serving the sports and entertainment niche are attracted to the glamor, prestige, and status of being among the "inner circle" of some of the worlds' most successful people. They also are attracted to the money.

If you are honest with yourself, you will probably cite at least one of these reasons for wanting to work with athletes and entertainers.

But before you jump off the cliff and land in la-la land, let's slow down for a minute and dig into the real opportunity that lies ahead for those who enter this niche with the right motivation.

If it were easy to break into this niche, everyone would be doing it. There are different challenges for different industries and different people, but anything worth having is worth working for. If you have the right work ethic and determination, you will be able to build a successful practice.

Aside from the glamor, establishing a practice working with this niche will help make your business more resistant to economic downturns. Like other wealthy people, sports and entertainment figures are less affected by economic shifts. They tend to be more financially resilient and spend equally in growth phases *and* recessions, often seizing opportunities in economic downturns.

Once you establish trust, these clients often repeat and can become an annuity of business for years to come.

If you have a firm or work for a company, a sports and entertainment division can lead to benefits for the entire organization. The prestige permeates company-wide.

In real estate, celebrity-owned properties can act as magnets for media attention, which benefits all clients who have listings with the firm. Non-celebrity clients and their listings enjoy elevation to greater visibility, which can help speed up the sales cycle and increase profits.

Many wealth managers who service the sports and entertainment niche make a point to connect their high net worth clients with their athlete and entertainer clients. Both find it beneficial. The athletes like making the business connections for potential off-field and post career opportunities. The non-celebrity clients enjoy meeting the athletes and entertainers and often will explore strategic partnerships with them.

Even if you're in business flying solo, you will elevate your profile by your affiliation with this caliber of clientele.

Is Sports and Entertainment the Right Niche for You?

One technique you've probably heard of for analyzing business opportunities in a given market is a SWOT Analysis, where you first look at the Strengths and Weaknesses you or your company bring to the table and then analyze the Opportunities and Threats that exist in the marketplace.

I find it is better to look for opportunities and threats in the market first and end with an examination of your strengths and weaknesses in how you will respond.

The way I see it, it doesn't matter that you have a great product or service if there are no clients who want it. It is better to satisfy a need or solve a problem that exists (even if people aren't currently aware it exists) than to launch a product or service for a non-existent market. So, let's do a SWOT analysis the OTSW way.

Opportunities

The opportunities to launch or break into this niche are numerous, but not every business is a match for the sports and entertainment client. Remember, athletes and entertainers have some unique needs.

Since they don't always have the time to research and handle certain business in their lives, they are accustomed to relying on the expertise of others, which means they often find service providers by referral. Once you build a steady stream of referrals, the business may ultimately find you instead of you having to search for the business.

Some questions you can ask to test the Opportunity are:

1. Is this niche being underserved in my field?
2. Would I be the first, or one of a few, to service this niche in my industry?
3. Do I need geographic proximity to service my clients?
    - If so, are there a lot of athletes and entertainers in my area?
    - If not, do I have a way to connect with them? Online?
4. Who do I know, or where could I go to help me create a flow of referrals?

The other part of analyzing the opportunity in your market is the numbers. Is there a market for this niche in your field or your industry?

It is better to satisfy a need or solve a problem that exists (even if people aren't currently aware it exists) than to launch a product or service for a non-existent market.

There are 32 teams in the National Football League (NFL) with 53 players each for a total of 1696 active players. When you add the active players from the 30 NBA teams (15 players each), 30 MLB teams (40-man rosters), and 30 NHL teams (23 active-man rosters), you have a total of 4,036 active professional athletes in the four major professional sports. This number does not include other significant sports that could produce clients. A colleague of mine has made a career of servicing professional soccer players from the European leagues. One of my attorney friends specializes in UFC fighters. There are also pros in golf, tennis, rugby, extreme sports, and more. Yes, you can have a niche within the niche, but sports and entertainment is specific enough to start with for now.

The number of people in the entertainment industries is considerably greater. Besides all of the actors and actresses, musicians, and other creative professionals, there are also all of the other contributors to those industries, including but not limited to: directors, producers, writers, editors, agents, managers, and more.

You will have to do some research to find out the numbers for your area. The number of potential clients will also dictate how much of your resources to dedicate to building this niche. If ten different people in your industry are competing for the same five celebrities in your city, then you may want to reconsider your decision to focus on sports and entertainment in that city.

Threats

An obvious threat to your business is someone else who is breaking in or already servicing the same niche as you. Don't let this intimidate you. Even if someone else has started before you, there are always ways to do it better. You can even learn from the mistakes they have made before you make them. It may be easy to duplicate the product or service you deliver, but the method by which you deliver it can be the thing that gives you a competitive edge.

Don't be intimidated by the degree of your competition's market share. The statistic can be deceptive. In real estate, for example, "dominant" market share may mean 8-10% of a specific market. That leaves 90% of the market to go after. Just because you see the competition's advertising the most does not mean they own the entire market.

There are also people who have one or two celebrity clients but have not built a specialty practice to service the industry as a whole. You may have the opportunity to be the first to do so.

Also, be aware of other not so obvious threats that may affect your industry as a whole or the specific requirements in servicing the sports and entertainment niche. For example, when dealing with high profile clients, it can be especially important to have clear boundaries and expectations laid out in written contracts around issues such as privacy, payment terms, non-disparagement, deadlines, and many other potential quagmires. Whatever your terms, make sure they protect both you and your clients.

Another example of an external threat would be technology. Could technological advances replace or threaten your value proposition? If embraced, technology can often enhance the experience you give your clients. It can also increase the efficiency.

You may be able to address most threats from the onset or avoid them altogether by asking the right questions. Here are some key ones to get you started:

1. Who is your competition? Has anyone else already created a sports and entertainment-focused practice in your area?
2. What are the threats to your industry as a whole?

- Is technology a threat to what you do?
- Can an online option replace your product or service?

3. Are there aspects of the financial climate that could affect your business?
4. What terms do you need to put in your contracts to protect you and your clients?

Once you have looked at opportunities and threats and concluded that sports and entertainment is a viable niche in your marketplace, it's time to look at you and your business to see how well positioned you are to serve it.

Strengths

Knowing your core competencies, or those of your company is critical to matching and enhancing them to the needs of the clients you aim to service. Your firm may have a strong enough brand to create immediate credibility and trust. If not, you must fill all gaps you can see in your core product or service before launching your sports and entertainment practice. You only get one chance to make a first impression.

> **There are also people who have one or two celebrity clients but have not built a specialty practice to service the industry as a whole. You may have the opportunity to be the first to do so.**

Here are some questions to help you see your strengths.

1. Why would it benefit an athlete or entertainer to work with you over all the other options?

- What makes you (or your firm) uniquely equipped to compete in the sports and entertainment market?
- Do you have a unique product or service that is ideally suited for this niche?

2. Do you have experience in sports or entertainment, even if it is limited?
    - Do you have a close relative or friend in either field?
    - Not just an athlete or entertainer connection, but anyone who deals directly with athletes or entertainers?
3. Do you have better access, resources, technology, or something else your competition or future competition does not have?
4. Is there anything proprietary about your product or service?

Weaknesses

If you're not aware that you have any weaknesses, you're in trouble. Even the best of the best have areas where they can improve. You should constantly be looking for how you can evolve your core competencies with an ever-changing business environment and your greater understanding of the wants and needs of your customer base. Being able to adapt to the changing needs of your clients quickly will keep you ahead of your competition, but you can only do that when you can see your weaknesses.

Additional research and training can overcome many weaknesses. Or you can fill some voids by calling upon the strengths of your team members, or by forming strategic partnerships with other individuals or firms. Partnering with those who have complementary skills can help complete the value proposition you need to win clients.

Questions to uncover your weaknesses:

1. What are your shortcomings when it comes to servicing the sports and entertainment communities?
2. What challenges will you face as you attempt to enter this niche?
3. Are there any certifications or qualifications you are missing that could add to your legitimacy in your industry?
4. What are you NOT doing that you know would create an excellent experience for your clients?

FOCUS & FINISH TIP:

Spend more time on pushing your strengths to the level of unfair advantage, and delegate your weaknesses to others.

Other Considerations

You must understand the market you are entering. Is it a new market or an established one? Will you be introducing the sports and entertainment or luxury niche to your market? Will you be competing with existing specialists and need to focus on differentiation? Of the number of potential clients, how many of them are viable clients for your product or service? Do they have to live in your city? Do you have to interface with them directly? Do most of them already have someone providing the same service you are offering? To how many of them can you actually gain access?

Spend more time on pushing your strengths to the level of unfair advantage.

Only you know the answers to some of these questions and taking the time to answer them will let you know if you are heading in the right direction.

Also, the number of potential clients may not have to be as high if your profit per client is high. Real estate is a value, not a volume, business. If the value you provide is high enough, then each deal pays out a higher rate, so that the volume will not matter as much. I know several business managers and agents who make a living with one great client. Also, focusing on the value you provide to your existing clients opens the door to other new business that may come from your affiliation with athletes and entertainers.

Be Sure You're Ready for the Majors

It is important to remember that although you may be new to the sports and entertainment niche, you can't be new to your industry and expect to service this top tier market. The handpicked members of my sports and entertainment division all had to have a minimum number of years in real estate as well as specific sports and entertainment experience.

Before you build your specialty practice, be sure you have a baseline level of expertise. Just like baseball players who train in the minor leagues before they get invited to "The Show," make sure you master the fundamentals before you approach professional athletes and entertainers for business. Know the contracts, rules, regulations, laws, or any other material information you must understand to serve your clients well.

Once you have figured out the basics of delivering excellent service in general, then you can begin to understand the unique needs and wants of athletes and entertainers; you can then identify the additional skills you need to develop and the new products and services you need to offer to work with this niche. The good news is that all this information is obtainable.

Benefits of Specialization

Almost everyone already knows someone with a real estate license. The barriers to entry for real estate are very low, too low in my opinion because too many people who are unprepared to handle large transactions get into the industry. This creates the need for specialization.

You may also be in an industry with low barriers to entry that appears to be saturated. It may seem you are competing with people doing a tenth of the business you do. You know you're way better at it, but these partial or part-time players in your market take up mindshare that could belong to you. They get one-time business that you could have turned into a long-term client.

When you commit to a specialty niche, you set yourself apart from your competitors. It becomes easier for the consumer to identify and remember you. It is better to be known as a focused specialist than to become lost in a sea of generalization.

Specializing also helps you increase your expertise. You discover more of the nuances as you encounter the specific challenges of dealing with your chosen niche. You also develop a better understanding of your clients' mentality and needs. More of the people you come to work with will also specialize in working with athletes and entertainers and will share their best practices with you.

For athletes and entertainers, work schedules, income flow, travel demands, privacy requirements, and other factors all add up to the need for an expert. That expert should be you.

If You Build It, They Will Come...

Systems and infrastructure help you deliver excellent, consistent service. It is imperative that you have these in place to service clients before reaching out or marketing to this niche. You typically get one shot with new clients, so you don't want to blow it. No matter how eager you are to get started, make sure all stages of engagement with a new client will demonstrate the level and quality of service you want to reflect in your business.

Make a list of all stages of interaction with a client, from initial engagement to close, and even to ongoing follow-up. This list can include everything from the first call, to follow up consultations, to product delivery. How is each step of the process unique to the sports and entertainment niche? How is your unique value proposition reflected? What in your materials or messaging will continue to reinforce your initial value proposition? Which systems for delivery will ensure you have a satisfied client every time?

In my business, the relationship usually starts with an introduction from a business manager or wealth manager. The steps we follow include an initial consultation, explanation of the process, and written restatement of what has transpired. Our goal is to make sure that every interaction reflects a level of service and follow-up that exceeds the client's expectations. Our materials look and feel top notch, and our follow-up is prompt and professional.

As a Division of an Existing Company

Creating an effective sports and entertainment division can be a huge value-add and a business magnet for a corporation, whether it be real estate, insurance, investment, or relocation services, to name only a few. When we launched the national sports and entertainment division for my current firm, it resulted in the most press hits the company had ever received. I have assisted multiple organizations in creating successful sports and entertainment divisions, and there are a few things to consider when launching under the banner of an established firm.

> **It is better to be known as a focused specialist than to become lost in a sea of generalization.**

Being able to lean on the reputation of an existing company can give you a head start in your niche. You can begin by offering services that include the core competencies of the company and add specialized services or products specific to the sports and entertainment niche. In this case, you are identifying the unique aspects of your company that align with the needs of the niche, and you are working to plug any gaps in service that exist.

Many companies are already starting to realize the importance of tailoring their services to meet the needs of the different clients they serve, and they are way ahead of their competition. Bespoke services geared towards everyone from teachers to doctors are becoming the norm. Retailers are now even able to target key demographics based on tracking social media preferences. Athletes and entertainers also have preferences and expectations that, if met, can lead to repeat clients.

If the company you work for is committed to the success of the division, you may receive a tremendous amount of support, and, if so, it will play an integral role in the success of your business.

It may also be helpful to align yourself with an influential person at your firm who can help you get the support and resources you need. You may not have direct contact with the CEO or key decision maker, but one of your close colleagues might. Get them on board first, and they may be able to make the pitch for you to present your idea. At a minimum, you will have a key influencer on your side.

FOCUS & FINISH TIP:

If you plan to approach your company with the idea of launching a sports and entertainment division, be sure to lead with how it will benefit the company. Demonstrate the specific revenue it will generate. Show how it will increase the overall visibility for the company.

On your own...

For those who plan to start a sports and entertainment practice and fly solo, there are pluses and minuses. On the positive side, you will have all the freedom in the world to create it exactly how you want it. On the other hand, you will have to create and finance everything yourself. That is possible, but you must be careful not to shortchange the quality of your brand. Instead of a brochure you print on your home printer, you may want to wait until you can afford a custom designed brochure on heavy stock paper.

Assuming you are carving out a sports and entertainment practice in a field where you already have experience and training, the key to your success will be your ability to market, sell, and serve these clients at the highest levels of excellence. Review the sections on branding yourself and your USP, then move on to packaging your services.

Look for others in your area, and online, who have a sports and entertainment practice in your industry. See what you can learn from the people who have been at it longer than you. Notice what they do well that you might imitate. Notice where you believe they fall short and make it a point to do better in those areas.

Check out their websites. Research and review what is working for them. Or as my friend, Tom Ferry would say, "R and D...rip-off and duplicate." Figure out how you can differentiate enough to have an unfair advantage or competitive edge. Also, don't rule out joining an established practice or acquiring an up and coming competitor. Effective mergers and acquisitions happen every day. You can learn a tremendous amount from working with the right person, and remember, 50% of something is better than 100% of nothing.

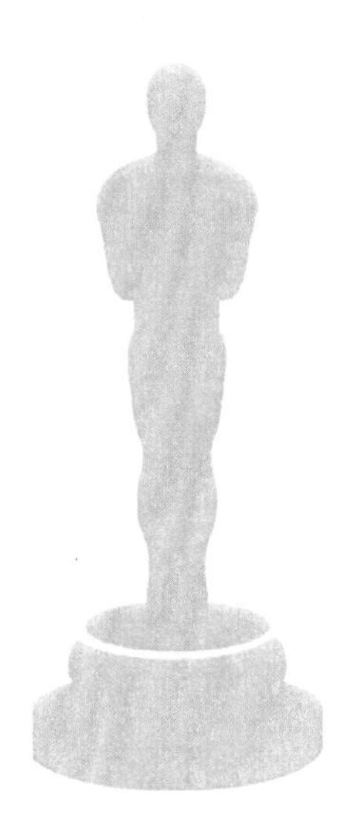

PART TWO

Selling to Celebrities

Selling to Celebrities

Start with Your Sphere

If you are just transitioning into this niche, it is important to tell everyone you know what you are doing. You can do a mass email blast, mail out letters, make personal phone calls, or host a launch party if you roll like that. I suggest a combination of some form of mass outreach, followed up by individual calls. It may take some time to reach everyone, but it will be worth it. It is often the personal outreach calls that lead to immediate business and referrals.

Keep in mind, people not only have to know what you do but they must be able to describe it to someone else for your messaging to be effective. If you have a business name, slogan, value proposition, or tagline that is easy to articulate, people referring you will also have an easier time describing your services.

FOCUS & FINISH TIP:

Try a quick experiment to test the effectiveness of your branding. Ask one of your close friends to describe what you or your company does. You might be pleasantly surprised when they give a better pitch than you, or you may receive a wake-up call when they can barely describe what you do. If they mention the job you had ten years ago, you have some work to do.

Make a Hit List

Make a hit list of ten to fifteen key centers of influence in the sports and entertainment niche in your area. Tell everyone you know who might be able to help you access important players on your hit list. Often, by telling people who I want to meet, or the type of person who would be beneficial for me to know, I receive personal introductions. Many of my key industry contacts have come through these introductions. Remember, everyone knows someone who knows someone.

> **If you are just transitioning into this niche, it is important to tell everyone you know what you are doing.**

Try to set up lunches, coffee, or meetings with these people. During the meeting, ask and listen for ways *you can bring value to them*. Notice I didn't say look for what they can give you. Keep your focus on how you can bring value to them or help make them look good to their clients. The most effective business building you can do is to bring value to others.

Find a Mentor

If you are just breaking into an industry and don't have a mentor, then you are mentoring yourself. That's like the blind leading the blind. Eventually, you will find your way around, but that could take years. Your competition will have left you in the dust, and you will be playing catch up. If I were starting my career over, the first thing I would do is find and engage a great mentor.

One way to break in is to find someone already working with athletes and entertainers and intern with them or work for them. You may have to work for free initially to gain the requisite experience. If you get the opportunity to intern for a leader in your industry who is already working the sports and entertainment niche, take it and make the most of it. Attend a conference or class on how to break into this niche, if there is one. I may even be coming to your city soon to teach a seminar. Check in on the "Sellebrity Network" website for upcoming events and training opportunities.

> **The most effective business building you can do is to bring value to others.**

For a busy, experienced veteran to want to take on a junior associate or intern, you must bring some value to the table. Ideally, you will add to the veteran's business or make life easier for them somehow. Figure out what value you can bring to a veteran in your industry. Maybe you can take some of the lesser tasks off their plate. Even better, you may have business or access to a business that the experienced person can help you close. I have also seen people leverage an existing friendship or relationship with a celebrity into employment opportunities. This usually comes with the promise that you can deliver that athlete or celebrity as a client to the firm. I often collaborate with agents who want to learn more about this niche and gain access to my Rolodex to promote their listings.

Building Your Farms

In real estate, agents usually work to build a client base within two kinds of "farms" - a geographic farm and a demographic farm. A geographic farm is a neighborhood or area that you already know or plan to know well, where you will focus your business. It is a measurable, manageable area that you can target and market to consistently. A demographic farm represents the type of client on which you have decided to focus. Examples of demographic farms in real estate include first-time buyers, short sales, condos, luxury homes, or sports and entertainment figures. Demographic farms may or may not have geographic boundaries. You may have to limit your geographic reach for athletes and entertainers depending on your industry.

You should base the size of your "farm" on a manageable number of contacts that you can market to consistently and effectively. This can be based on your budget and the type of outreach that best supports your industry. Are you sending mailers, utilizing email campaigns, or hosting client appreciation events? Answers to these questions will help you determine the frequency and expenditure required.

Positioning and Mindshare

When I first introduced myself as a sports and entertainment specialist in real estate, there were no other real estate agents or firms presenting themselves in my market this way. Today, in a market saturated by sports and entertainment "specialists," you've got to decide what you will do to stand out. It's vital that you communicate what you do and your unique value proposition (also known as Unique Selling Proposition, or USP).

Positioning

These days, marketing experts often refer to "positioning" more than USPs. Positioning can be described as the place a product or service occupies in a consumer's mind compared to the competition. Having a strong position is especially important in industries that are saturated with competition. If you want to own a permanent parking space in the consumer's mind, you must deliver your concise and consistent message frequently.

Going back to O.T.S.W., the key is being able to articulate your unique selling proposition that speaks to their specific needs. What makes you different from everyone else in your industry? What makes you uniquely positioned to service the sports and entertainment niche? What "distinctive mix of benefits" do you offer? Review your answers in the Strengths section to get some ideas.

Your USP needs to be clear, concise, and memorable. Your USP is a statement, promise, or marketing pitch that your competition cannot or does not make. One example is Domino's Pizza. Their promise was, "You get fresh, hot pizza delivered to your door in 30 minutes or it's free." This example is overused, but it is referenced so often because it was notably effective.

If you want to own a permanent parking space in the consumer's mind, you must deliver your concise and consistent message frequently.

Think of it as your elevator pitch. You must be able to deliver it quickly, in a way that people understand, and that they can easily explain to others. Here's a good test—your value proposition should be so simple a child could understand and describe it.

Whatever your USP is, it must also include a higher level of service and expertise for sports and entertainment clients. Your main service or product may be the same as others, but your combination of offerings and how you deliver them can set you apart. Remember, this niche can afford the best, so you must articulate why that is you. You must know the categories where you beat your competition and how to utilize that advantage.

Mindshare

Mindshare means if a consumer thinks of a name in a particular industry, the degree to which they think of yours indicates your amount of mindshare in the marketplace. It connects you and your value proposition to your product or service category in consumer's minds.

Either way you look at it, the key to positioning and mindshare is consistency with your marketing. Your message must be included or communicated in all of your collateral and marketing pieces. You will not achieve positioning and mindshare overnight. It will take time and will happen based on how consistent and memorable your message is.

Remember, this niche can afford the best, so you must articulate why that is you.

When people think of your industry, do they think of you? Are you the first person they think of, or are you one of many? If you are one of many, your niche may not be specific enough, or you may not be communicating it effectively. Make sure you state your competitive advantage in terms of benefits to your customers.

MARKETING MATERIALS AND COLLATERAL

When I first started in this niche, the rubber message wristbands were very popular (e.g., Live Strong wristbands). I made a batch of thick black wristbands with my mantra "Focus & Finish" subtly embossed in black on them. The URL for my company website was printed on the inside of the bracelet. These were extremely popular with my clients, athletes and entertainers alike. Many of them subscribed to an active lifestyle, and my message resonated with them. I could tell, because the next time I saw them, 100% of my athlete clients would be wearing the bracelet. These were easier and more fun to give out than my business card and had a lot more "stickiness" or memorability factor. Would they have worn a wristband with "Kofi, Your Realtor" on them? Not likely.

When considering which type of collateral or marketing products would be most effective for your industry, think outside the box and come up with something creative. Perishables, like food, drinks, and flowers are good on occasion, but I like to utilize things that have a longer shelf life.

Spend some time and money on creating your marketing materials and collateral. Your collateral must be of the quality one would expect for the type of clients you aim to serve. You don't have to have a long list of celebrity clients for your marketing materials to make it seem like you do. Everything about your business should look and feel like a luxury product or service that resonates with the sports and entertainment crowd. The colors and font can play into this, so do some research online on luxury branding. Your business cards, brochures, and website all need to come across as upper tier. The card stock you use is a simple place to start. Ask your printer about "soft touch" options for your cards. They are thicker and have a distinctive feel to them. Also, your other printed materials need to utilize professional photography, simple text, and avoid too many colors. The lives of athletes and entertainers often reflect a luxury lifestyle imagery that is both beautiful and aspirational. Try to capture these elements in a way that is appropriate to your industry.

When I started in real estate, I would compile the client's initial paperwork in a simple, plain folder that had a business card holder on the front or inside flap. It was neat, easy, and it worked.

Once I decided to pursue the sports and entertainment niche, I had branded folders made. They had my company name on them and the subtitle: "Specialized Services for Athletes and Entertainers." They were well-received and demonstrated my commitment to the niche. Also, I knew my clients' friends and associates would see the folders, which would help increase exposure for my brand.

For pitch meetings with high-level prospects, I would buy leather padfolios and had a silver nameplate engraved with the client's name and my company named underneath theirs. The cost was about $40 each, without any guarantee of a return, but they were very well received. Most people like receiving a personalized presentation, especially when it has their name on it. My conversion rate with the clients who received the personalized padfolio was about 75 percent. With an average property value of $2,000,000 and a 2.5 to 3 percent commission, it was well worth the $40 investment.

Protect Your Brand, Say No to Business

When establishing yourself in a new niche or business, it is hard to say no to any incoming business. You need to start making money or recoup the money you put into launching your brand, and it can be tempting to take on the wrong clients just so that you have some clients. In the infancy stages, all business may seem like good business from a moneymaking standpoint.

The truth is: not all business is good for your business. Some business has the potential to distract from or diminish your brand. I remember meeting a salesman who would refer challenging or time-consuming clients to his competitors. These "problem" clients would keep his competition busy while he focused on the more fruitful business. Before you jump on referrals from competitors, ask yourself, "Why don't they want that business?"

If you have to or want to take on clients that don't fit into your new branding, do it under a different brand or banner, or don't do it at all. See if you can refer it to a junior team member. You can still oversee the transaction, but won't have to be as hands on.

Focus & Finish Tip:

Don't make the mistake of focusing on the good, while missing out on the great.

Co-Branding & Strategic Partnerships

Find already established brands servicing this niche and explore opportunities to co-brand or form strategic partnerships with them. This method is a quick and easy way to benefit from their established brand identity and the quality and service it connotes. As an example, we will often partner with a luxury car company to host our open houses. They will bring a car from their dealership to park in the driveway. Having a cool car to check out helps attract our target demographic, and it gives the car dealership exposure to a new database of potential clients.

The truth is: not all business is good for your business.

Co-branding can help you gain credibility in this niche faster. You can co-host events, sponsor their events, or have them sponsor your events. Including their collateral with your marketing material may also be an option. Also, when you co-brand, you and your marketing partner can share databases. Doing this can help you increase exposure and awareness for both of your brands. Co-branding can be another great way to create unique client experiences.

To figure out which businesses to approach about co-branding, consider who has a complimentary, but not competitive, product or service that already serves athletes and entertainers who can refer business to you. For example, if you make custom shoes, look for a custom suit maker that works with NBA players. If you are an accountant, find a wealth advisor that works with NFL players. People who are not in competition with you are more likely to refer business. If your business augments theirs, you can become a key resource for them to refer their clients to, and you can also refer business back to them.

> **Before you jump on referrals from competitors, ask yourself, "Why don't they want that business?"**

You can also look for opportunities for vertical integration. It may make more sense for you to purchase or be acquired by another company that is part of the service or product supply chain for your industry. Such a strategy only makes sense if they have a similar target niche or access to the athletes and entertainers.

FOCUS & FINISH:

Identify two or three brands that serve similar clients to yours and represent the image that you wish to portray. Find ways to partner with them and adopt in your own way the best of their systems and branding.

It's Not Just Who You Know

We have all heard the saying, "It's not about what you know, it's all about who you know," as if somehow, by knowing the "right people," your phone will ring, your inbox will fill up, and opportunities will come flying your way. That just isn't the case. Who you know is only one part of the equation and is virtually worthless without three other key factors. If any one of these is missing, you will struggle to network and generate referral business. Let's take a look.

1. **Who you know**—Yes this is the first part, but only part. You have to have some connection to the right people, or at least access to them. You don't always have to know them well, but knowing them is better than merely knowing "of" them.

2. **Who knows you**—It's actually more important that your potential clients or referral sources *know you* than that you know them. If they don't know you, it is as if you don't exist. If a third party mentions your name, will they know who you are? Remember, mindshare is key.

3. **Who knows what you do**—It is not enough for them to know you. They must also know what you do. If they don't know what you do, they won't know to think of you when it counts—when someone they know is looking for someone who

does what you do. The worst thing to hear someone say is they wish they would have known what you do before they hired so-and-so to do the same thing.

4. **Who likes you**—Though it may seem trivial, being liked adds to being memorable, and that leads to being thought about for business. Likeability is a tricky science, but one of the keys is to show up with an attitude of being interested, rather than trying to be interesting. Ask people questions and learn about them. People are interesting, and they love to talk about themselves. Showing a genuine interest in getting to know someone will endear you to them.

Networking

Join a networking group, common interest group, alumni group, or any group with a membership that fosters referrals and information sharing. It should be more than just a social group. The people in attendance should be busy, working professionals, who only show up because there is value in the room, valuable conversations, and valuable connections. Groups of people with something in common are more likely to do business together. The common bond helps to establish faster rapport and trust. The right networking group can provide warm introductions in an otherwise guarded environment. There are already some that focus on working with athletes and entertainers. Try different groups, stick with those that work, and drop those that don't.

FOCUS & FINISH TIP:

If the right networking group does not exist, consider starting it yourself.

Networking is not about asking for business but about establishing relationships that will lead to organic business referrals. It is important for people to know about your business and what you do, but it is just as important for them to know you as a person. Remember, "who likes you" is a key factor. The more you connect with someone on a personal level, the greater the chances that they will refer business to you when the opportunity arises.

Networking is also about giving value. The people in networking groups that tend to get the most referrals are also the ones who give the most. Making good introductions for others in the group can establish you as a well-connected important person to know. Take time each week to think about connections you can make for people. There may be synergies between people in your network, and you should give them a chance to explore what business can get done. Because you thought of them, they will be more inclined to make connections for you or find business referrals to send your way.

Networking is not about asking for business but about establishing relationships that will lead to organic business referrals.

Charity events are a great place to network and meet athletes and entertainers. Many of them have their own charities or attend the charity events of others. Sometimes you can find sponsorship opportunities. I once sponsored a lane at a charity bowling event for $250 that ended up leading to $125,000 in commissions over the following six months. As with other networking opportunities, keep the focus social and let the connections build organically. You will always make more connections talking sports than talking sales.

Be A Resource, Get Publicity

By being a resource to your clients and others in your industry, you can position yourself as the go-to expert in your field. Reach out to local, regional, and national news sources and offer your expertise. Journalists are always looking for experts to quote for an article or TV news story.

A couple of years ago, I was invited to speak on a panel at a national convention for luxury real estate. The audience was comprised mostly of journalists and resulted in over fifty national newspapers, journals, and blogs quoting me. Over the next six months, I was contacted over a dozen times and asked to provide quotes in real estate related articles. The media exposure was great for my business and for building my reputation as an industry expert.

Write blogs or articles and share your expertise as it relates to the sports and entertainment niche. What is happening with the celebrities in your area? What information would be valuable for them to know?

Don't write gossip articles, but do provide value-packed information that resonates with potential clients and other professionals in your industry. But be prudent: athletes and entertainers are often big on privacy and will not want to worry about being front-page news by working with you.

Online/Social Media Presence

The following phrase has become cliché, but remains true: "An online presence is as important as ever." Even if your clients don't find you online initially, they will eventually view your online profile. This profile starts with your website and trickles down through mentions of your name and any social media in which you participate. Google yourself and see what comes up. You can't control all the content, but address anything that doesn't support your professional image. The goal is that your prospects see content that supports and elevates your status as a sports and entertainment specialist, not the embarrassing photos from that house party in Cancun. (Unless you were partying with celebs!)

You will always make more connections talking sports than talking sales.

Social media has also become a unique way to connect with people with whom you desire to do business. LinkedIn is one way to make business connections and find people with similar or overlapping business models. You can use it as a tool to find other people in your industry or other industries who work in the sports and entertainment niche.

Social media also continues to grow as a viable avenue for promotion, advertising, and lead generation. Look at your pages like a client would and ask yourself, "Would I hire my social media profiles?" If the answer is no, you have some work to do on improving your social media image.

Be very strategic with what you post. You have to have acceptable ratios of business and personal posts. People don't want to be bombarded with ads. They also like to know something about the person they are working with. Informative, social, and comedic interaction are often met with fewer objections than direct solicitations or selling.

Facebook allows the option to create a business page. With a business page, you can "boost" your posts, allowing you to reach specific demographics based on areas, interests, age, and more. For a nominal fee, your post will show up on their timeline, even if you are not friends or connected with them on Facebook. I have seen favorable results from my boosted posts - everything from more incoming calls to increased traffic at open houses. One of the stories I tell at my seminars is how I once sent a direct message on Facebook that lead to over $100,000 in commissions from that one client over the following six months.

Business Begets Business (Referrals)

Every client should lead to at least two new contacts for more clients. When you are in a transaction with an athlete or entertainer, you should always come away with at least two new potential sources of future business.

Every celebrity has an agent or business manager. They have accountants and wealth advisors. They may even have a cook, trainer, a hair stylist, or other professionals they work with regularly (all potentially great referral sources). Get to know as many of these people as you can during your time servicing your client. Make time to meet with these people in person. Add them to your contact list. If they are serving one celebrity, chances are they have more clients just like the one you are working with. If you treat them well, they will refer other clients to you.

Make Gatekeeper Connections

Gatekeepers can be the toughest to break through to, but also the most fruitful connections. Sports agents, business managers, financial advisors, CPA's, publicists, and attorneys have several, if not dozens, of clients that may need your product or service. Even individual sports teams usually have someone on staff to assist the players with their off the field needs. They are often the central referral source for everything from real estate to where to buy groceries. If you can connect directly with these industry gatekeepers, you can create referral sources that can fuel your entire career.

The best and easiest way to connect with a gatekeeper is through a personal introduction. Go back through your sphere and ask if anyone has made any of these contacts and can make an introduction. Remember, these gatekeepers get inundated with solicitations, so even an introduction by a friend must be compelling. Your friend must also see the value to the other person in making the connection.

Every client should lead to at least two new contacts for more clients.

If you have exclusive or proprietary information that would be beneficial to them or their clients, then you have a reason to share it. The key here is that the information is specifically valuable to the sports and entertainment niche, and is not readily available to the general public. If the connection or their clients can access the product or information on Google, then the perception of a special value may be lost.

For example, in real estate, I will often send my sports and entertainment contacts a scoop on a property coming up for sale before it hits the open market. This "heads up" gives them a chance to share exclusive information with their clients and gives their clients a chance to purchase the property discreetly before it becomes public information. Even if the property or timing is not quite right, they appreciate being in the know.

FOCUS & FINISH TIP:

Think of the exclusive or proprietary aspects of your business that pertain to the sports and entertainment niche, and find creative ways to share them with the industry gatekeepers.

Get Certified as a Specialist

As part of the membership process for our sports and entertainment division, agents are required to go through a training program that focuses on the practices and principles that apply to a sports and entertainment transaction and how do deal with the different people involved in the transaction. I have created a certification program that will be available to our Sellebrity Network, as no other program currently exists. This training will give people a certification to use while marketing themselves in this niche.

Pricing and Fees: Know What You Are Worth

Pricing is a key component of most marketing strategies. Don't try to win business by being the low-cost leader. Just because you can beat your competitors on pricing for your products or services does not mean you should. Catering to this niche is not the time to lead with low costs. It is the time to lead with high value.

Athletes, entertainers, and other affluent individuals associate quality with price. They expect to pay more for higher levels of expertise, experience, convenience, service, and quality. But you must deliver with tangible, better service, and higher quality products.

Our firm once took over a listing to sell a luxury home development that was struggling. As part of our repositioning strategy, we actually encouraged the developer to increase the prices. The buyers they were trying to reach did not see any alignment between the price point and what they would typically pay for other luxury products or services. If you don't set prices high enough, the quality of a product can be called into question.

Don't focus on competitive pricing, focus on the quality of the service or product you provide, because that is what the athletes and entertainers will focus on. Once there is enough competition within this niche within your industry, it will either push prices down, or the benefits within the offering must increase. That is a basic principle of economic supply and demand and the push towards perfect competition. As supply increases, the competition for the existing demand also increases. If consumers see you as the same as your "competition," you have not done a good enough job separating yourself and your value proposition.

Some will resort to lowering their fee structure. That is the easy way out but is usually just a temporary solution. I encourage you to stand by the value you offer. Be willing to improve your offerings and increase your value, but don't take the shortcut of discounting your fee. Be sure to read the chapter on Market Domination to gain a defensible head start on your competition.

Don't try to win business by being the low-cost leader.

Like Attracts Like

Make sure you align your strategy for differentiation with the mindset of the high net worth individuals you aim to serve. For example, never try to own the market as the low-cost leader. Wealthy individuals are accustomed to paying higher rates for higher quality products and services. They also expect the higher levels of quality and customer service that accompany these costlier purchases. Lower prices may hurt your ability to sell to them because they often associate a cheap rate with lower quality. It is important to value your product or service.

It is only when you value your service, that others will too.

Dress to Suggest = Dressed for Success

Your personal image must align with your business's brand. How you dress makes a statement. Make sure you're not a walking contradiction to the brand image you wish to portray.

Take a look at the people who are successful in your field. Note how they dress, how they present themselves, what kinds of cars they drive, where they hang out, and where they go out to eat. Modeling yourself after successful people can be a great way to help you create alignment with how you want others to perceive you to take your business to the level you want.

Your wardrobe is an easy place to begin, but before you go out and buy a $5,000 Armani suit, make sure it would appeal to your audience.

While people like to make friends with someone they can relate to, they like to do business with a person who presents as a professional. When I first meet with my athlete and entertainment clients, I rarely wear a tie but often wear a suit. By our fifth or sixth meeting, I may show up in jeans, a button-down shirt, and designer tennis shoes if we are meeting in a more casual setting.

When I took my first multi-million-dollar listing in Manhattan Beach, CA, I showed up to my open house looking very professional in an Italian suit, perfectly knotted tie, and Magnanni shoes. Great for Beverly Hills, but I was completely out of place in the beach culture.

As agent after agent walked into my open house in shorts, sandals, and Hawaiian shirts, asking me where I was from, I realized just how out of place I looked. In the beach towns, even the luxury real estate agents tend to dress casually. It fits the energy of the area, and clients looking for beachfront properties relate much better to that style of dress. I may never show up to an open house in a Hawaiian shirt, but I will definitely leave my tie at home.

Besides place, also consider with whom you're meeting. While a suit without a tie is usually a safe bet, sometimes a suit and tie can make your audience feel uncomfortable. Business managers and agents may respect the shirt and tie, or business suit, more so than an athlete or entertainer would. For women, mastering the in between look can be a little more challenging. I have seen some pull off the look successfully with a skirt or dress and the right pair of heels. Sometimes, slacks may work well too. Another tool for women is wearing quality accessories. The key is to convey a level of professionalism along with a comfortable, relaxed presentation. Finally, also try to stay one step ahead of your client. They can dress extra casual, but that may not be as appropriate for you.

How you dress makes a statement. Make sure you're not a walking contradiction to the brand image you wish to portray.

My acting days taught me to dress the part when auditioning for a new role. It is always important to keep an element of yourself incorporated in your presentation. Unless it's part of your style, don't go out and buy cowboy boots for a meeting with a cowboy or country western singer. That will make you look ridiculous. Maybe you wear jeans to the meeting instead.

If you don't yet have the budget for the Armani suit, another strategy is to mix in an expensive item or two in with your more modestly priced clothing. For men, you might wear a pair of special, custom made shoes or a nice watch. The right timepiece can often make the subtle statement you need to convey - an air of luxury or success.

For women, a nice, identifiable handbag can do the trick. A Fendi or Chanel purse conveys success and can create a little healthy bag envy. The other nice thing about an individual statement piece is that it can be subtle. When your Cartier watch peaks out from under your sleeve, or your Damier Louis Vuitton Artsy is draped over your arm, people will notice.

Even when you are off the clock, how you dress can benefit your business. If your job is anything like mine, anyone you meet is a potential client or can refer clients. Make a point to wear clothes that people can connect with or discuss. This can mean sporting a t-shirt from your Alma mater or favorite sports team. You can even wear a shirt that has your birth city on it or a cool international destination that you have visited. Clothing that sparks conversation can do some of your networking for you.

Clothing that sparks conversation can do some of your networking for you.

Use Sports & Entertainment Tools for Selling

The sports and entertainment industries provide us with useful tools that we can apply to business. Some of the basic principles that lead to success in athletics and entertainment are transferable to business, even if you have never played sports or worked in entertainment. Also, if you implement some of these strategies, your athlete and entertainer clients will recognize them and feel more of a connection with you.

Tools from Sports

Teamwork: Your industry may function or feel like an individual sport, but every salesperson should have a team. The team starts with the firm you work with or the infrastructure you create. Your firm's reputation and resources can make a huge difference in the successful launch of your business. You can build on this reputation and utilize the resources to launch a sports and entertainment based practice. It is hard to launch as a one man, or one woman, show. It is even harder to service the clients without support. Utilize existing relationships and support staff in your organization.

From the administrative staff to the CEO, every employee reflects the company culture and contributes to the client experience.

Your team also extends to your key vendors. Make sure to meet with these key vendors regularly to ensure a holistic experience for your clients. There should be a feeling of seamless synergy between you and your preferred vendors. The client should feel like their services are just an extension of your own. These vendors may be able to tailor the service they provide for your clients to be more reflective of how you do business. For example, I have a lender who tailors his initial and follow-up emails to reflect being part of our "team."

Your spouse, family, and friends are extended team members. They support you with encouragement, time, and energy, and maybe even filling in when your assistant or other employees can't. Be sure to let them know you appreciate them. When I close a deal, my wife gets a bonus too. This makes those long workdays and open houses on the weekends a little easier for her.

Hard Work and Discipline: In sports, we know that outworking the competition is one of the keys to success. We spend the time and energy necessary to give us the best chance at winning. Athletes practice their craft to perfect their skills. The same ought to be true in business.

Be willing to put in the time and effort to achieve the goals you have set for yourself. Be disciplined and work hard on what directly correlates to success in your business, namely sales. Keep in mind that hard work is useless unless it is also smart work. Spend time on the aspects of your business that yield the greatest results.

Practice: Top-notch athletes spend hours practicing, but salespeople often forget the importance of mastering their craft. What should you practice? Know the scripts and dialogues for your industry. Read and reread any forms, documents, and contracts that relate to your business. Go online and research updates and trends in your industry. This practice must be consistent and ongoing.

Athletes practice for hours every week, and often every day, all in preparation for game day. I often refer to my client meetings as "game day" because it's the reason I have been practicing. I am ready to deliver my pitch or proposal with confidence. If you can, find someone with whom to practice. A coach or mentor may be an option, but if not, at least find an accountability partner for the same purpose. Schedule a regular time to review and rehearse the materials for your field. Practice builds competence, and competence builds confidence. Confidence is comforting to your clients.

Keep in mind that hard work is useless unless it is also smart work.

Knowledge and Creativity: One of the greatest NFL running backs, Barry Sanders, once said, "I ran with my ability, but I also ran with creativity."

We marvel at how some of today's athletes are doing things in their sports that we have never seen before. The top salespeople in the country are also landing and closing deals in ways that are unique and impressive.

The stronger your grasp on the fundamentals, the greater your ability to innovate, improvise, and get deals done. First, you must know your industry inside and out. How are others in your field getting deals done? How can you make deals happen or service your clients in ways that others can't?

In the legal system, they say there is the letter of the law and the spirit of the law. In business, the spirit of the deal is often more important than the letter. Get creative, satisfy the spirit of the deal, and then back it up in writing with the letters of the contract.

FOCUS & FINISH TIP:

Learn the fundamentals; then apply your creativity. You must know the boundaries of the box in order to think outside of it.

Know Your Competition: In sports, coaches and athletes spend significant amounts of time studying their competition. They watch game film of the opposing team in preparation for going into battle against them. The bottom line is they go to great lengths to gain an edge on the competition.

While we hope it's friendly competition, competition exists in almost every industry in business too. You have to know who your competitors are in your industry in general before you begin to build your sports and entertainment practice. You have to know who is doing what and how they are doing it. You will also want to know who, if anyone, has already started to focus on athletes and entertainers. Where do you fall compared to the competition? Do they offer more or less than you? Is their presentation more professional than yours? Do they have a head start on market share? You can overcome all of these things, but you must know where you stand in relation to the others in your space.

The other thing to remember about competition in business is you aren't just competing with other people or companies, you are competing with resources on the Internet and other options consumers have at their disposal. Technology can disrupt an industry overnight. How can you work with

> **Confidence is comforting to your clients.**

the existing technology or create a defensible position around your product or service that cannot be replaced by some new invention? Stay on top of the information that is out there. Technology should be utilized to support your core competency or offering, but should not be the only part of it. For example, if your industry relies on research, technology should make that research easier to obtain and more available for your clients.

Use your market knowledge to stay ahead of whoever or whatever you are competing with. Superior knowledge of your market or industry also creates an advantage. Stay on top of the trends to stay ahead of your competition.

Dealing with Losses: Handling setbacks is one of the most important skills you can learn from sports. In sports, you can use a loss as motivation to improve. For example, more than any other position, cornerbacks in the NFL are taught to have a short memory. If they get beaten on one play, they have to shake it off and be ready for the next play. Feeling the pain of loss can also inspire off-season efforts to improve so as to avoid feeling that pain again the following season.

In business, we lose deals, clients, negotiations, commissions, and more. Yes, each loss hurts. But don't hold on to these feelings because they will only distract you from the successes ahead. Win or lose, figure out what you are supposed to learn from every situation and move on.

Finally, remember you have to lose some to win some. Even the most successful venture capitalist knows that for every ten companies they invest in, only two to three are expected to be a major success. It's a numbers game.

FOCUS & FINISH TIP:

Embrace the feelings associated with the challenges you face. Just don't let them become roadblocks. Be sure to use them as learning opportunities and building blocks towards success.

Have Fun: One of the main reasons people play sports is because it's fun. The same should be true of your work. The more you know about your job, the easier it will be, and the more you will enjoy it. The more you enjoy what you are doing, the better you will be at it. Working with athletes and entertainers can be challenging, but also a lot of fun.

The idea that work can be fun may seem oxymoronic, but you have to find the fun in what you do. Part of this is finding the sweet spot between what you are good at and what you like to do. Even if much of your job is challenging or difficult, there must be other aspects that are satisfying and rewarding.

In my job, I truly enjoy the personal interaction with my clients, negotiating deals, and coming up with creative marketing strategies to get properties sold. These areas are where I focus most of my efforts, and my business has grown because of it. I always try to deliver good news in person, because I like to see the smiles on my clients' faces. I don't cheat myself out of these rewarding moments by sending an email or text when I don't have to.

Tools from Entertainment

Learn Your Lines – I learned through my years in acting that knowing the lines is important, but bringing something extra to those lines is more important. Lines are just words on the page. You have to know something about who your character is and something about who you are talking to in order to deliver the best line. You have to be aware of the situation, the needs of the person, their state of mind, and the right timing.

> **The more you enjoy what you are doing, the better you will be at it.**

The more experience you have, the more the "lines" become your own, in acting and sales. Even before the actual experience, you can improve your skills through practice. Take the time to rehearse. It will pay off when you have the one opportunity to land or close that big sports and entertainment client.

What are the lines you must learn to dominate in the sports and entertainment niche in your field?

Be Creative – Most successful actors improvise very well. This ability comes from experience and practice. In most industries, there are fundamental skills and knowledge that you must have to do any business at all. Once you have command of this foundational information, it becomes easier to think creatively and to work things to your and your client's advantage.

With athletes and entertainers, you can use creativity to gain business and get deals done. Improvising will help you manage a deal even when your clients' lifestyles and schedules are all over the place. You have to be able and willing to pivot on a dime. You have to be prepared to bring creative solutions to challenging scenarios and problems.

We all bring a multitude of experience and skills to our jobs. Don't be afraid to bring your experience from a different industry or pastime to your field. You can apply techniques and tools you have learned in another field or industry to your current job or sports and entertainment based practice.

FOCUS & FINISH TIP:

Interdisciplinary approaches to problem-solving can produce the best solutions.

Dress the Part & Show up Camera Ready – As mentioned earlier, know your audience and dress accordingly. Also, show up looking professional. Different clients may warrant different looks or styles, but make sure you put in the effort. Try to stay one step ahead of your client, but not three. What I mean is if your client always shows up in ripped jeans and a t-shirt, you may show up in regular jeans and an untucked dress shirt. A suit may be overkill depending on your profession. For other clients, it will always be important to show up in a suit and tie.

Act the Part – Act like you would behave if you had worked with 20 different celebrities last year and did a record amount of business. Don't wait until it happens. Act as if it is already your life. Coming from a place of success and confidence is more effective than working from scarcity.

Also, don't oversell. If you are spending too much

time trying to convince your client on why you think something is right for them instead of why it is in alignment with their goals, then you may be overselling. I have discovered there is a correlation between the increase in price and less need to sell. Some clients need lots of guidance, while others like to make decisions on their own. The only time you should sell your client is if you are selling them on what they already said they wanted from the beginning, and they just need a reminder. In this case, selling is merely reiterating how the good or service will meet the needs or desires they have expressed.

FOCUS & FINISH TIP:

Celebrities, athletes, and high net worth individuals like information, not persuasion, to inform their decision making.

It's a Numbers Game – In acting, you may audition dozens, maybe even hundreds of times before you land that part that changes your career. The same may be true when building your client base. You may land several roles as a co-star or guest star before eventually landing a lead in a feature film. This preparation, however, will get you ready for the bigger opportunities. Opportunities to pitch or sell your product may be few and far between, so seize each one on this journey toward your goals.

YOUR BRAND – A PROMISE TO YOUR CLIENT

Your brand usually starts with a name, sign, symbol, design, or combination of these things that represents you or your company. It typically serves as a quick, unique way for people to recognize you or your company. Your brand symbolizes a promise. A promise of what customers can expect when they utilize your product or service, both tangible and intangible benefits.

Often, your branding is the first thing people will see. It creates an initial impression, so it should evoke some type of emotion and may directly or indirectly relate to the product or service you provide. In this niche, emotions related to trust, security, and luxury come to mind. The branding should be intriguing enough to capture their attention and informative enough that they know what you do.

As a new division or company, your brand should be easy to understand, if not through your logo, through your text. The Nike swoosh would be meaningless without the history and success Nike experienced. This is even truer of the Michael Jordan Jumpman logo. Because of Jordan's proven success and track record, it has become a true symbol of achievement and one of the most recognizable brands in the world. Both brands are able to drop the words associated with them because the symbols have become recognizable.

People should not have to work to figure out what you or your company does, or that you focus on sports and entertainment clients. Your logo, name, and description should make it clear what you do. Even if your company name is abstract, the subtitle or tagline should communicate what you do. As your market share and brand awareness increase, you may be able to just use your logo for some of your advertising.

The client's experience that follows will create the ultimate, lasting, impression of your brand and dictate the values that people assign to your brand. It is where you deliver on the promise of your brand. Things like expertise, reliability, responsiveness, and confidentiality should be among the values that come to mind. The athletes, entertainers, business managers, agents, and others will have a certain impression of you and your service based on how they feel as a consumer. The experience the client has while interacting with your brand or engaging your service will lead to brand loyalty and brand equity. Once you have established these two things, consumers will automatically assume and assign the values you have demonstrated to anything to which your brand is attached. As soon as they see your name or your logo, they feel a certain way and make assumptions about the experience that will follow. They know what to expect from your brand.

This expectation is why it is important to examine all the different touch points you have with your clients - from the introduction to acquisition to completion of sale or service, and for some, providing ongoing service. Each touch point provides opportunities to demonstrate or reiterate your value proposition. If part of your value proposition is responsiveness, then each interaction with your client should be prompt, complete, and include expected and unexpected follow-up to ensure thoroughness.

With the sports and entertainment niche, your brand should resonate with athletes, entertainers, and their gatekeepers. Aspirational imagery reflecting the wealth and the experiences that accompany it often represents the world of luxury. The affluent get exposed to products and services that often reflect higher levels of quality or service. Almost everything about the way these products and services make the client feel can be described as exclusive and special. This concept is well executed in travel magazines, car commercials, and ads for clothing. The imagery often sells the desired lifestyle that stirs emotions. You may feel in awe or amazed.

Your brand symbolizes a promise.

In real estate, we use photos, videos, and language to create emotional responses to properties. We then follow up with market information, lifestyle opportunities, and comparable properties to justify the value on a rational level.

Keep in mind; sometimes the simplest approach can be the best. Your sports and entertainment division may be best described as simply, "The Sports & Entertainment Division." There are a lot of values and assumptions built into the words "Sports & Entertainment" or "Luxury." This built-in value can work to your advantage.

After wrestling with several overly creative names for the new real estate division we were creating to specifically service the sports and entertainment niche, we ultimately decided to call it the "Sports & Entertainment Division." It wasn't glitzy or clever, but it said it all. At one of my previous firms, I was the director of the "Luxury Homes Division," which also was the easiest and most accurate way to capture our value proposition. Even now, my firm's "Global Sports & Entertainment Division" succinctly communicates who we are. These titles specifically state the specialty and capture the assumptions we desire.

Having a value proposition that you communicate often will make it easier for your clients and prospective clients to remember you, and your branding should reflect this proposition. Building your brand takes planning and a long-term commitment. To obtain the brand recognition you desire can take years. If you shift away from your consistent marketing and messaging too soon, you can lose all your hard work. You can start by surveying people on your brand. Ask them how it makes them feel? What does it make them think of? Is it communicating the right values to the right audience? This feedback can prove invaluable. The San Diego Chargers quickly learned this lesson in their move to Los Angeles. They launched a new logo that was very similar to the Los Angeles Dodgers logo, and it met immediate backlash. They immediately withdrew the logo.

If you are not getting any traction from your branding in three to six months, you may want to reevaluate. Just keep in mind that traction can be as simple as people saying, "Oh, I've seen your logo before."

A Calling Card for the Rich

A sports and entertainment niche practice can quickly become a means for other wealthy individuals to find you. There is a lot of overlap between the lifestyles of athletes, entertainers, and other high net worth individuals.

Most athletes and entertainers have access to the best products and services available, so if they choose to work with you, reason dictates that you must be one of the best. The credibility that comes from working with celebrity clients can get you in front of other prospects and lead to more referrals.

Emotions Rule

Most buying decisions are made emotionally and justified intellectually. People buy based on how they feel or how they think they will feel once they have made the purchase. Even large financial decisions start with an emotional response and are later supported by logic or facts. Your brand should produce some emotional response or connection for athletes and entertainers.

Trust is usually the biggest factor for selecting business professionals. If you can evoke a feeling of trust, you are halfway to earning the business. In real estate, a positive emotional response to a property is one of the most powerful factors in making a buying decision, so we focus a lot on trying to create an emotional desire to own the property. Then we follow up with factual information about the property and its value to justify the initial emotional response.

Questions to consider: What emotional triggers influence the selection process for choosing someone from your industry? What factual information will back up the emotional response that is initially triggered by your brand?

FOCUS & FINISH TIP:

Your brand should have emotional and rational components.

The Appeal of An Exclusive Feel

Celebrities and affluent individuals want to feel special. Their wealth and success have afforded them access to what I call the "Chauffeur Driven" life. They have to know they received access to a product or service that others can't access. It must feel exclusive.

Whether as part of another company or on your own, you must separate your upper tier marketing from your regular marketing. It is easy to find examples of brands that have a top shelf, black label, platinum club, or another upper tier offering. The American Express Centurion Card, also known as the Black Card, is a perfect example of this.

When I made the decision to focus my business on servicing athletes and entertainers, I knew I would have to brand myself as exclusive. When a prospect looks you up or goes to your website, you have to show why you are the right choice. Prospects should feel like you are the best and maybe the only person that can meet their specific needs. You must brand yourself as the premier sports and entertainment expert in your field.

I decided to invest in a website that would be my calling card for the client base I was aiming to reach. I spent $10,000 creating a custom website that presented me as an expert in sports and entertainment real estate. By no means do you need to spend that much money on a website to get started, but because of the prominence of the Internet, make sure that your website shows well. It should be clean and fairly simple, with high-resolution images. My site focused on the benefits of working with a sports and entertainment specialist. It was flashy, with great images, and screamed luxury.

You may not be in a position to jump right into the sports and entertainment niche or upper tier market. You may need to maintain your more modest client base while building your roster of more affluent clientele. This creates the need for the distinction. One of the ways that I did this was by keeping two separate phone lines. For my luxury real estate voicemail, I had one of my British cousins record my outgoing message. Her voice was perfect. Something about the Brits suggests refinement and luxury. My close friends got a kick out of it. They joked and laughed (as did I at times), but it resonated with my clients and those I aimed to serve.

Most buying decisions are made emotionally and justified intellectually.

I guarantee you won't be complaining if you add other affluent clients to your practice, in addition to your sports and entertainment clients.

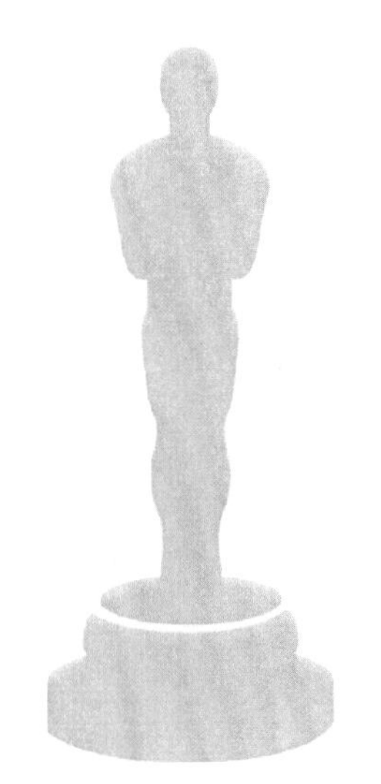

PART THREE

Servicing Celebrity Clients

Servicing Celebrity Clients

Deliver Excellent Experiences

For you to succeed in serving this elite group of individuals, it is not about looking at what you can *get* from this niche, but ultimately it is the degree to which you develop the value you can *bring* to it that will determine your success.

Affluent individuals are often afforded and have become accustomed to personalized tailored experiences. The best-known luxury brands already understand this and have adapted their client experience accordingly.

You may offer a similar product or service as others in your industry, but these days, the product or specific service you offer is only a minor part of the equation. In the rarified air of sports and entertainment, the client *experi-*

ence is becoming more important than ever. People who pay premium pricing are paying for the experience. Your job is to make sure your clients' experience is first class.

Look at Virgin Airlines, a company that built its entire brand on creating an extraordinary flying experience, and people pay their higher airfares to receive it.

In the rarified air of sports and entertainment, the client experience is becoming more important than ever.

This is the same credo behind flying first class. Everyone gets to the same destination at the same time, but those who fly first class are paying more for a higher level experience.

Be Like Suede

When asked which personality traits make for success working with clients in the sports and entertainment niche, I always tell people to be like suede. Suede has several characteristics that apply to working with this clientele.

Suede is a type of leather, so it is tough. Toughness is an important quality in being an advocate on behalf of your clients. Most industries are full of predators who target athletes and entertainers. You will often find yourself in a position where you need to protect the best interests (and the bank accounts) of your clients. We must be tough enough to stand up and fight for our clients when necessary.

Suede can also be soft and smooth. Sometimes, you have to be delicate in dealing with your clients. You may also have to finesse a negotiation or transaction to get the desired results. Many of our services or products are big-ticket items, so emotions often come into play.

Managing these emotions can require a balance of being soft, yet firm. You will have to mirror and match your client's style to create rapport. Sometimes you must be resolute and bring your client into alignment with how they need to think and which actions they need to take to get the best results. Sometimes you have to roll up your sleeves to get your work done, and other times you will need to be more hands off.

Bottom line, suede is versatile, and you will have to be too if you are going to be successful in this niche.

Location, Location, Location

The location of your office or business can also contribute to the image or perception of your brand. As a luxury real estate brokerage, having a location in Beverly Hills has its advantages. The 90210 zip code is recognized globally as an affluent and glamorous area. Even "online real estate" has become expensive. At the time of this publication, URL's ending in dot luxury (.luxury), come with a minimum $800.00 premium.

While a physical location in the most desirable part of town or on the most desirable street may initially cost a prohibitive amount, a virtual office may not. You can pay for a virtual office, which gives you a physical mailing address in a location you desire for as little as $100 per month. Even "We Work" has some great locations with memberships starting as low as $49/month. This often comes with access to meeting and conference rooms if you need them. A phone line and receptionist are even part of certain packages. They will answer the phone stating your company name and forward the calls to your cell phone or another remote location.

Make sure your location is relevant to your brand and is close to or where you conduct business. Certain industries like real estate, personal trainers or pet care are better served and more readily received when exhibiting a sense of local expertise. Sometimes it is important to know the local influencers and win them over first. If it is important for you to know the local landscape, make sure you do.

Understanding the Client

It is important to understand the mindset and culture of those you aim to serve. You may have played amateur sports, never played sports, or have not one athletic bone in your body. You may have done acting in high school or college, or the closest you have come to the entertainment industry is a 3D movie experience at IMAX. It doesn't matter. There are still ways to learn about athletes and entertainers, what they value and how they think. Understanding their work, game, and travel schedules is a great place to start. If an actor films in another city for 3-4 months out of the year, most correspondence may have to be digital. You may have to travel to get deals done in a timely fashion. You may need to alter your schedule to be available at odd hours or inconvenient times.

In addition, not being from these industries can give you a unique perspective that you can bring to your clients. Think of it as an inter-disciplinary approach to servicing them.

Whatever your unique background is, your experience can contribute to your value proposition. Athletes and entertainers don't expect you to be like them, but understanding something about their world can help you relate better. It can also help you tailor your services to meet their specific lifestyle needs.

I once spoke on a panel at the Beverly Hills Board of Realtors on cultural diversity. We discussed diversity (or the lack-there-of) within the luxury industry, but also the different cultures we serve. I made the point that there are more than ethnic or racial cultures to consider when determining the most effective way to deal with a client. There are also demographic, geographic, psychographic, and socio-graphic cultures, to name a few. For example, their careers often ebb and flow; athletes can have careers cut short by injury (i.e., yours truly). The sports and entertainment niche has its unique characteristics. Even within the niche, athletes are different from entertainers. For example, as groups often targeted by salespeople, they can be more guarded.

A Different Playing Field

Way back in the eighties, the TV show *Lifestyles of the Rich and Famous* gave us a glimpse into celebrity lifestyles. Now we have reality television, celebrities posting on social media, and TMZ to give us an even closer look. Ironically, the privacy we help our clients protect is often exposed, and we can use that information to begin to understand the lifestyles of the affluent. Just by following a celebrity on Facebook, Twitter, or Instagram, we can see how they live, what they like to do, and with whom they like to hang out. This insight can help provide a greater understanding of how to cater to their wants and needs. I am not suggesting cyber-stalking a potential client; just use it to gather some baseline information.

THE "CHAUFFEUR DRIVEN" LIFE

People don't hire a chauffeur because they don't know how to drive. They hire a chauffeur because they want to have a certain kind of experience and their time is better spent on other things. They may have work to do, calls to make, or it may be their one opportunity that day to relax and enjoy the ride. Their income affords them the opportunity to live this way, so they take it.

Look at your celebrity clients' lives. See which aspects are chauffer driven, meaning, note which services or responsibilities are typically taken care of for them.

Actors and athletes are accustomed to a pampered life. Even in my modest acting career, I flew around the world first class, was chauffeured to and from locations in luxury cars, stayed in four and five-star hotels and frequently ate at fine dining locations.

During my *very* brief time as a wide receiver with the Oakland Raiders, I recall the numerous vendors that catered to the athletes. We had suit makers, jewelers, and even luxury car dealers who would bring their products to us at the practice facility. I use the collective "we," but they were usually catering to the top draft picks and high paid veterans. I recall a $250,000 Ferrari being dropped off to one of the guys for a week-long test drive.

Even when we traveled, someone took care of everything for us. Chartered planes, catered meals, and ground transportation were all provided. The goal was for the athletes to be able to focus on what was important and that was the game. Everything else was handled by someone else.

You must allow your clients the same peace of mind — the business they transact with you will be taken care of without a hitch, with as little involvement from them as possible. Make it a priority to do your job in a way that removes the majority of stress from your client and lets them focus on their craft or career, and you can have a full roster of clients at all times.

The same "chauffeur driven" life is essential in the entertainment world — sometimes even more so. Service for this niche often reinforces the status of these individuals. They are looking to you to make them feel important. Make sure you give it to them. They will appreciate knowing they are in the hands of an expert who knows what they need and provides it without a hitch.

People don't hire a chauffeur because they don't know how to drive.

Our concierge service offers everything from movers to staffing. A relocation client can arrive at a house that is fully furnished, fridge stocked, and their clothes color coordinated in the closets. This service allows them to focus on work and family instead of the headaches of moving.

How can you make your client's life easier? What concerns, challenges, or stresses can you remove from their lives through your services or during the process of working with you?

Not All Celebrities are Alike

Assuming that all "celebrities" are the same is like assuming that all "sports" are the same. Football is different than baseball, just as athletes are different than entertainers.

Athletes

For many athletes, their first contract is their introduction to being rich. Many arose out of lower economic conditions. They have spent most of their athletic careers as amateur athletes when they had to refuse pay to maintain their amateur status. Their new pro status sets up a dramatic shift when the first signing bonus or paycheck comes in.

The money and lifestyle a professional sports contract brings are usually new to them. These things influence their lifestyles and buying habits. They will often play catch up by buying lots of the things that eluded them pre-riches. Shoes, cars, clothes, and jewelry frequently top the list. They also may feel pressure to keep up with the other guys in the locker room. Their teammate gets a new car, so they want one too. The challenge is this same teammate may have a $20 million contract, while the rookie is working from a $500,000 contract.

Also, the assumption is that the money will never end. Rookie athletes are young, in the best shape of their lives, feeling invincible, and assume they will have a long career. Their spending reflects this belief, but it is rarely the case. For example, according to the NFL Players Association, the average NFL career is a mere 3.3 years.

Depending on your industry, you may have an opportunity to provide guidance on which service or product would be best, based on the stage and uncertainty of your client's career.

For instance, in real estate, the decision is often about whether to rent or buy. The best decision for most athletes on a new contract moving to a new city is to rent. If they want to buy a property, it should be as an investment, or in their hometown where they will spend their off-seasons.

Consider which long-term versus short-term decisions athletes would need to make in your industry. Be prepared to advise them well.

Make it a priority to do your job in a way that removes the majority of stress from your client and lets them focus on their craft or career.

In addition, the athlete mentality is often one of collaboration and teamwork. They understand what it means to be part of a team and to carry your weight. You must be able to convey to them how you and your team work and how you will be able to service their needs effectively. This includes your ability to work around the demands of their lifestyle. For example, I sometimes use a clause in my contracts that keeps my athletes from being penalized if there are delays in signing documents due to game or practice schedules.

Athletes are usually creatures of habit, and more importantly, creatures of their teammates' habits. They work out, eat, and practice on a schedule. Knowing this schedule can guide you in finding the best times to reach them or meet with them.

Many players seek referrals from their teammates. Athletes spend hours together on and off the playing field. Therefore, it is important to maximize each opportunity. If you can take care of one player, you will often get a referral to his or her teammates.

NBA stars are fewer in numbers, so they are often afforded more individual attention and may require more hands-on service. NFL players are often well taken care of and well paid but have less notoriety due to playing behind a helmet. They may not have to deal with as much attention from the general public unless they make a lot of off-the-field appearances. They are both recognized by their stature. Recognition has its pluses and minuses. We cover this in the section on "Famous: To be or not to be." These things can affect how and where you meet with your clients or the expected experience for each interaction.

Research your existing clients and ideal future clients and keep a dossier on each one of them. You should know as much about them as possible, but at the same time, don't assume you know what type of person they are. Knowing something about their background, career path, likes and dislikes, and other Google accessible information can be helpful when used appropriately. But nothing will tell you more than being seated at the same table with them.

Understanding your client ahead of time can help you tailor their experience of working with you. On the other hand, assuming you know them based on what you've read online can keep you from getting their business. Also, even if you feel like you know them from what you have read or seen on television, they don't know you.

Be genuine in your approach, get to know them for who they are, and give them a chance to get to know you. Consider this recommendation for entertainers, too.

It is important to be yourself; many athletes and entertainers have a sharper sense of recognizing con artists and others who aren't who they pretend to be.

Entertainers

What may appear to be overnight success probably is a result of years of hard work, dedication, and loads of rejection. Most entertainers struggle for some time before they earn enough to make a living. By the time they have made it "big," they often have a greater appreciation for their newfound wealth. Many are conservative at first about spending it, due to the uncertainty of when they'll get their next project or gig.

Like athletes, entertainers expect a collaborative effort. It takes dozens, sometimes hundreds of people to bring a project to life. During my acting days, I always marveled at how many people were working behind the scenes to set the stage so that we actors could "bring it home." Entertainers understand the importance of each person having a role and being very good at what they do. Once you demonstrate your expertise in your field, they typically trust you to assist them.

Most successful entertainers have an agent, business manager, stylist, personal trainer, and more. Each service provider has a specific role, and the entertainer relies on each individual's expertise. Focus on being an expert in your role, but also be able to work with the other key members of their team. Relationships with business managers and agents are critical to your success in this industry.

Different industry professions present different needs and requirements. The lifestyle of a television actor is very different from musicians who may be on tour for half of the year. A writer may not have all of the same privacy needs as a famous actress. Again, these are just generalizations, and you should evaluate each client individually. The best way to understand a client's needs is to ask.

Levels of Wealth

The Institute for Luxury Home Marketing separates the wealth accumulation curve into three categories: Apprentice Wealth, Journeyman Wealth, and Master Wealth. As people transition through the different stages, their understanding and appreciation of wealth also transitions. Their spending habits and propensity to spend also shifts. It is important to understand how these habits tie to your industry and how you can best service your clients based on their stage or category.

While it is true that affluent people tend to think and operate differently than the middle class, it's also true that there are differences between the millionaires and the billionaires. The newly rich behave differently than the established "old money" wealthy.

Understand that among the affluent, wealth and the amount of disposable income will vary, and you will need to determine how this influences how you market to and serve them.

Many wealthy people, especially those from long-established wealthy families, have their money tied up in investments or family trusts. They are wealthy on paper but cash poor. Those newer to wealth may have more cash at their disposal, and will often be your best spenders. It's not just that they have money, but the propensity to spend it, that can make for a better prospect.

The best way to understand a client's needs is to ask.

Talk, Text, or Tweet?

It's important to know the right platform to reach your clients, and consistently market to them in a way that gets you in front of them while it resonates with their lifestyles. Emails, handwritten letters, phone calls, social media, and texting can all be highly effective or wildly inappropriate, depending on the client.

Consider age, background, experience, lifestyle, and industry the client works in as major factors that contribute to how they prefer to communicate. Most of my millennial clients are avid texters, but my baby boomers prefer email. Deliver important information by phone or email; texting can be okay for messages or quick questions that need a rapid response. Social media can even be an effective method of outreach on occasion, but only by private messaging. Public mentions or solicitations almost never work.

One of my NBA clients was tough to reach by email, difficult to reach by text, and almost impossible to reach by phone. He would, however, respond to messages on Twitter.

The bottom line is, ask your client how they prefer to correspond. This will help you avoid communication missteps, which could lead to losing a client.

Where to Find Business

When I started my sports and entertainment division, one of the first things I did was join several professional associations. I joined sports agent associations, sports manager associations, and talent manager associations. They each charged a nominal annual fee and gave me access to their database of contacts. Soon I was a member of several national networks for sports agents, business managers, and any other web-based organizations that allowed membership through a credit card payment. I then took the time to copy and download every contact from every organization I joined. That proved to be slightly better than useless. That's right, useless. #EpicFail

A cold industry contact is almost like having no contact at all. Because of their status, or the clients they represent, these people are contacted with pitches and offers all the time. I was no different from anyone else trying to tap into their Rolodexes for business.

Now I am in the same boat. I constantly get bombarded by requests from people who want to form strategic partnerships to gain access to my client base. The main calls and emails I respond to these days are from warm introductions. Look for a way to bring value to the people you want to reach and even better, try to get a warm introduction. Reaching out on your own is different from someone introducing you as a person they "need to meet." LinkedIn has become another great place to get warm introductions. It does half the work for you by identifying common contacts and connections. Also, you can ask for an introduction via email. Finally, warm introductions can come from finding common ground. What do you have in common with the person you want to meet? Did you grow up in the same area, attend the same school, support the same charity, or have similar hobbies? Any of these could be the first step towards a warm introduction.

Your Team

One of the most important aspects of preparing to work in this niche is making sure you have the right team in place. Athletes and entertainers have demanding needs, and it typically takes a team to make sure all their needs get met at a level of service that is second to none. Each member of your team is a reflection of you and your business, so they should all understand, agree to, and implement your standards for how you want your products and services presented.

You may already have employees or may be hiring them for this new venture. Either way, they will need to be vetted to be sure they are qualified to service these types of clients. Past experience servicing high-end clientele is a huge plus. Experience dealing with athletes and entertainers is an even bigger plus. You want people who put the client and the service first, even before themselves. That does not mean subjecting yourself to verbal abuse, or cruel and unusual punishment. It does mean, however, going the extra mile for a client. Even as a manager with my firm, I once went out to buy sheets and towels for an NBA client for whom we had done a lease. His flight was landing at 10 p.m., and he wasn't going to have time to pick up these basics. I went the extra mile on his three-month lease, and a year later I picked up the listing on his multi-million dollar primary residence.

Discretion is also important. Every person I hire is required to sign a confidentiality agreement that protects my clients and their personal information. We often deal with very sensitive information, and every member of your staff must handle it with the utmost care. Privacy is one of the most used terms in this industry for a reason.

Finally, members of your team can't be star-struck. In this niche, your staff will get the chance to meet high profile athletes and celebrities. The last thing you want is for them to ask for a picture or autograph, or do anything else that is inappropriate. They must stay professional at all times. Behaving in an appropriate manner goes for you too. These people already get more of that kind of attention than they want; the last place they expect to get it is within their inner circle.

Don't worry, do your job and there'll be plenty of opportunities for photos and more importantly, testimonials. As long as you aren't overly eager or act as though you expect them, those opportunities will come when you deliver great service, exercise discretion, and demonstrate professionalism.

Keys to a Successful Transaction & Future Referrals

Once you obtain the client, how you deliver the service will often dictate the success of the transaction and whether or not you receive future referrals. You don't want to drop the ball. While there are many factors at play, the following characteristics are what I have observed to be the most important to this niche.

Be an Expert

Expertise is number one on the list for a reason. Celebrities want to know they are working with an expert. They reached their level of success by being an expert at what they do, and they can afford to hire the best for any services they need. Knowing your industry inside and out will play a critical role in advancing your career and separating you from others trying to work this niche.

An important thing to realize is access to most information is greater than ever, especially with tools like Google. It is your command of the information that will set you apart. What information do you need to have a command over to be considered an expert in your field for the sports and entertainment niche? You may already know a lot about your product or service, but how does this knowledge apply in the worlds of sports and entertainment?

The advice and guidance you give your sports and entertainment clients should demonstrate your knowledge of your industry in tandem with an understanding of theirs.

For example, I often write a provision into my celebrities' leases that allows them to have someone present when vendors (handymen, plumbers, housekeepers, etc.) have to do work on the house. That helps prevent security breaches or photos of the celebrity's home from turning up in the media. Consider the unique needs of athletes and entertainers who utilize your service.

Stay Up-to-date.

Always stay on top of trends in your marketplace or industry. Your clients shouldn't know about advances in your industry before you do. Even if they happen to read or hear about it first, it is your job to interpret it for them.

When your opportunity comes, when you get called off the bench, you need to make sure your skills are tight. If your opportunity strikes and you are not ready to perform, you may not get another opportunity for a long time. Pick two to three key sources of news in your industry to read every week. At least one should cover your local market. Another should cover national trends. Finally, you should refer to some source that covers new and best practices.

FOCUS & FINISH TIP:

Identify three quality sources of professional information to read weekly.

Be Professional

Be on time. Be responsive. Be proactive. All of these contribute to your professionalism. Professionalism may seem like a no-brainer, but you'd be surprised how many people don't even master these basics. Professionalism starts from your first contact with a new client and continues through the end of the transaction.

Timeliness is critical. If you are not early to an appointment, you are late. If you are on time, you are late. The client can be late (and often will be), but you can't. The next section discusses being flexible, but timeliness is also part of professionalism and must be a top priority.

It is also very important to be responsive. With busy lives and schedules, when clients have questions, they often need a quick response. You don't always have to have the answer on the spot, but at least respond to let them know you are working on it. Then, get them the answer as quickly as possible.

In my industry and several other sales industries, the biggest complaint consumers have had regarded a lack of responsiveness. It is critical to respond promptly.

Finally, being a professional also means not being a fan. I have received invitations to numerous concerts, games, and events of my celebrity clients, but only because I've never asked.

> **If you are on time, you are late.**

Be Flexible

There is the saying that time waits for no one ... except celebrities.

Celebrities' schedules change faster than the weather. Be ready for last minute calls, cancellations, rescheduling, and explaining to other professionals why your client is running "a few minutes behind."

Being flexible will make working with celebrities a more enjoyable experience for you and your client. Due to their hectic schedules, I often give my clients a fifteen to twenty-minute cushion on their actual appointment time. If the scheduled appointment is at 2 p.m., I will ask them to be there at 1:45, and they will usually arrive at around 2:15.

Also, remind your friends, family, and loved ones of the need to be flexible. The same flexibility that allows you to work from home on occasion also means late and/or odd hours to meet the demands of your clients. It is often a trade-off, but the good far outweighs the bad. This trade-off is especially true when your hard work allows you to treat yourself and your family to a great lifestyle.

On one occasion, I received a call from a business manager saying their client will be flying into town in about two hours and would like to preview as many houses as possible. Even though it can be a challenge to produce results at the last minute, your mindset must be, "Let the games begin." See it as an opportunity to separate yourself from your competition.

Another time, I successfully set up six last minute previews for my client only to have his arrival get delayed by a day. Well, "let the games begin"...again...tomorrow!

Dealing with Business Managers, Agents, and Family

Whether it's a business manager, agent, friend, or relative, find out all the individuals who will be influencing the celebrity's decision making. It might even be a pet. (Candy Spelling had her dog Madison help her pick her real estate agent.) Work closely and professionally with these key contacts. Treat them like you would treat the celebrity.

When possible, it's easier and more efficient to have all decision makers there at the same time. Sometimes this is not possible. Then you have to find ways to loop in the other decision makers as quickly as possible. When showing homes, clients or their trusted advisers will often use Facetime on their cell phones to bring the other decision makers into the room. Conference calls may work for your industry or another form of technology.

> **Being a professional also means not being a fan. I have received invitations to numerous concerts, games, and events of my celebrity clients, but only because I've never asked.**

If your client does not want anyone else involved, you must respect your client's wishes. It is best for the client to relay this information. You may have an unhappy person on your hands who may actively work to disrupt your transaction if you are just ignoring these peripheral people or telling them they can't be there.

If you treat the business managers and agents well,

they can end up sending you future business and referrals. Most of them have several clients, and they like to know their clients are in good hands. Once you have done a great job with one client, you can lobby to be their preferred vendor for that industry.

Even after you have identified all of the key influencers, you must also understand their motivations in the transaction. Their goal may be to protect the client from any and all risk. It may be hard to get this person's support until they know you are also trying to protect the client. They may be financially motivated or have other self-interests factoring in.

I had a past client whose "business manager" was previewing all of the properties for him. I use the term business manager lightly because it was more of a friend who helped him with a few business affairs. This friend was vetoing homes that I thought were perfect for the client. It wasn't until I found out that he was going to live with the client that it all made sense. The next house I showed him had an amazing guesthouse in addition to the other desired features. He said this is perfect, recommended it to the client, and the client bought it. Know the intentions of each decision maker.

There is the saying that time waits for no one ... except celebrities.

Be Discreet

Athletes, entertainers, and other celebrities value their privacy, especially with their business dealings. All of my team members and staff have to sign Non-Disclosure Agreements to work with me. Our clients grant us access to their homes and financial information, and we must protect this information with the utmost care.

Also, their work lives tend to be public, but they prefer that their personal lives stay off the radar. It is respect for this privacy that helps build trust and opens the door to more business. I am visible and outspoken in my industry, but my client's personal business ALWAYS stays private.

Famous: To Be or Not To Be

Depending on circumstances, to get the work done, you may or may not want to utilize your client's celebrity status. You and your client get to decide if it makes sense. Between you, you can base the decision on the product or service you are providing and the industry you are in or by the degree to which you want to control the media spin that may come along with the action.

Advantages: *Easier Access, Preferential Treatment, Quicker Response Time, Better Service*

In the business of real estate, particularly when selling a property, there is the decision that you must make whether or not to disclose that the owner is a celebrity. There are several factors to consider.

On the one hand, revealing that the owner is a celebrity can bring additional publicity to a property, and exposure is a huge marketing tool. Numerous media outlets are looking for stories on celebrities, and you can use that to your advantage. You can also leverage sharing the information to build your media relationships. Giving exclusive or first access to stories can endear you to media sources and give you some control over how the story gets conveyed to the general public.

> **I am visible and outspoken in my industry, but my client's personal business ALWAYS stays private.**

When given the green light, I have used the celebrity status of my clients to promote their properties and at the same time, their upcoming movies, charities, special interest stories, or other information they would like to share with the general public. I have used my television appearances in a similar fashion. The exposure is great for my business and me but can be equally beneficial for my clients who wish to promote something about themselves.

I once sold a house for former NFL running back and Hall of Famer, LaDainian Tomlinson. I took over the listing of his amazing property in San Diego. It had been on the market for over three years with other agents but had not sold. It had received some organic media coverage based on it being his house, but his popularity was not deliberately used to stimulate interest. With his permission, I created marketing that highlighted the property and the fact that he owned it. I strategically reached out to my preferred media connections first (media connections I established the same way I have instructed you to do) and they wrote stories about the house. Through media syndication and our other marketing efforts, we were able to get the house sold in two weeks! This method is just one of several examples of how I have used this to create a win-win-win for all. This story also helped me land the listing on LaDainian's Texas home AND later land Michael Jordan as a client.

Another advantage is the preferential treatment that accompanies celebrity status. People tend to be more accommodating and willing to go the extra mile for celebrities. Letting them know with whom you are working can sometimes get things done faster, with an increased level of service.

Disadvantages: *Price Gouging, Paparazzi, Loss of Privacy, Negative Public Perception.*

Sharing your client's celebrity status isn't all sugar

and spice. There are also disadvantages of which to be mindful. Sometimes, when vendors hear the words athlete, entertainer, or celebrity, the asking price "magically" goes up. People see dollar signs and think they can charge more simply because your client has the money to spend. You may have to choose between concealing your client's identity or arguing the price down.

I once had to have one of my NBA clients' house cleaned before putting it on the market. When the cleaning company found out whose house it was, they wanted to charge four times the normal amount! I quickly called their business manager to cancel the service call and hire one of our trusted vendors. The cleaning company was not happy, but the client was ecstatic that I saved him money. Protecting the client earned me future business from the business management firm because they knew I was looking out for their clients.

Another disadvantage to revealing celebrity status can be attracting paparazzi and losing privacy. Discretion can be critical in protecting the privacy of your clients. You can avoid unwanted media coverage and allow for some level of normalcy for an otherwise highly publicized existence by being discreet.

Your client may be a great person but have a negative public image. If this is the case, it may hinder getting certain access or services. I have had a few challenges during my career getting people to lease to certain clients who had reputations for partying a lot. We were able to overcome these challenges, but it often hinged on my reputation or an increased security deposit.

Your Vendor Network

As a real estate broker, I have been called on to refer everything from interior designers to a company that installs tennis courts. Be sure you have trusted, professional vendors with a track record of working with high profile clientele in your Rolodex (by Rolodex, of course, I mean smartphone). I refer to my group of preferred vendors as my "ecosystem." An ecosystem is defined as a group of living organisms interacting as a system.

For best results, nurture and care for your ecosystem. It is even a good idea to meet with your ecosystem routinely. As you all get to know each other better, your transactions will become continuously smoother. Also, as you send your vendors more business, they are more likely to do favors for you and your clients. The vendors in my network all go the extra mile for my clients and me, whether that means working late, accommodating my clients' demanding schedules, or facilitating unique requests. You too should go the extra mile for your vendors.

Keep a stable of vendors in each field to match different clients' personalities. Some clients will want someone direct and to the point. Others will want someone who is going to explain every step of the process while holding their hand and rubbing their back. You won't always be able to use your preferred vendors, but try to do so as much as possible. I usually like to provide my clients with two choices for the service they require. I have my top choice, but I also have back-up options. Always keep your eyes and ears open for new and better partners. I have my favorites, but the battle for the second option slot is ongoing. Look for vendors who not only will service your clients well but ones who become strong referral sources for you. Be honest in your goals for the partnership:

You don't want them receiving referrals from you while they are sending people you could serve to someone else.

FOCUS & FINISH TIP:

Create and nurture your Ecosystem.
Meet with them regularly.

Deliver

You can waste all of your efforts and make everything you have learned in this book meaningless if you don't deliver on the promise of your service or product. You must be an expert at what you do, and part of that is knowing how to get deals done and deliver quality products or services. People are not going to hire you just because you are a nice person. They expect you to deliver.

As an expert in your field, you should have the hard and soft skills to get deals done and solve the unique problems your clients have. Deals are not always straightforward, especially for athletes and entertainers. You have to know the nuances of your industry that will allow you to get difficult deals done, which will separate you from your competition. Developing a consistent record of producing expected and unexpected results will lead to raving fans and future referrals.

Always remember to communicate your deliverables up front. This way, your clients will know when you have delivered on your promise. That is the best way to manage expectations and exceed them when you can. Also, if you can't complete the job for some reason, you can show everything you have done and possibly earn another opportunity.

I once had a listing that didn't sell within our six-month listing period. Because I delivered on everything I promised, the client knew it was not through my lack of effort that the property did not sell. They renewed the listing with me, and I sold the house two weeks later. That would never have happened without communication and documented efforts.

BECOME A TRUSTED ADVISOR

Can you offer value beyond your specific profession? Are you connected to other people or organizations that would be good for your sports and entertainment clients to know? Do you know professionals who provide ancillary services to yours and who have experience working with athletes or entertainers? Once you provide a high level of service to your client, they may ask you for referrals for related or unrelated services. You can become a trusted advisor, and it will benefit you to have relationships with other top-notch service providers as part of your "circle of trust."

You have to know the nuances of your industry that will allow you to get difficult deals done.

POSTSCRIPT

Postscript

7 Keys To Market Domination & Keeping Your Edge

Once you successfully launch your practice, others will look to create a similar one. They will want a piece of the sports and entertainment pie. Consider the old saying: "There is enough business for everyone." Well, I treat business like I treat dessert, I want my unfair share. I have a sweet tooth for desserts and an unrelenting desire for business success. I prefer both in large portions.

Success in this niche often comes with visibility; your competitors will see what you are doing. As I mentioned earlier, most information is available online, including yours. They will think they can do what you are doing and do it better. That may become true if you don't look for ways to continue to dominate your market and keep your competitive edge.

Keeping your edge in any industry is about creating a highly defensible position.

Initially, the most common advantage for a new business or service is speed to market. If you can be the first to market and establish yourself, others will be playing catch up. In business, this is called a first mover advantage. It also depends on the barriers to entry, and unfortunately, there are not many barriers to entry for some of the services the sports and entertainment niche will buy. Anyone who wants to call themselves a specialist can. However, this does not mean you can't outshine the competition and keep an unfair advantage in your market.

I have a sweet tooth for desserts and an unrelenting desire for business success. I prefer both in large portions.

Lean heavily on your unique value proposition. Remember, only you have your unique combination of experiences and skills. Package and market them in a way that is difficult to duplicate. New entrants to the market will have a harder time duplicating what you are doing the more unique it is.

Here are seven keys to get you on your way to market domination and keeping a sizeable head start on your competition:

1. Know The "Players."

ALWAYS pay attention to the competition; know who they are and what they are offering. You can't stay ahead of your competitors unless you know what they are doing. They may be copying what you are doing or may have an innovative approach that you can duplicate.

At least once a month, do a search to see if there are others looking to enter this niche or have entered already. You will be able to view their website and any other online marketing they are doing. What is their lead value proposition? Is it similar to yours? Are they coming up in Google searches ahead of you?

It wouldn't make sense to lose out to the competition because they have copied your basic model and only tweaked it slightly. It does make sense, however, to do the same to your competition. Look for ways you can do what they are doing, and do it better. Don't be afraid to add features or services that are working for the competition. Rest assured, the smart ones will be doing the same thing to you.

Once you have established yourself in the market, your messaging should shift to reinforcing your unique value proposition and reassuring your client base that they should continue to work with you. After you have done a few deals, you will have social proof to reinforce your claims of effectiveness. Closed deals, industry recognition, and testimonials are examples of social proof that validate your brand. They do not mean that you should stop marketing to new clients, but keeping the clients you have and getting referrals will become more of a priority over time.

You should always look for ways to keep your competitive edge and build on the head start you have established. You must continue to innovate, while still keeping the core values and commitments that built your business. This leads us to the next point, evolution.

2. Evolve: Always look for new ways to service your customers.

A moving target is harder to hit. Your business model should constantly be evolving to stay ahead of your competition.

Anticipation means staying ahead of your client's wants by providing them with conveniences before it occurs to them to ask. Anticipation is not as simple as it sounds. It requires research, feedback, creativity, and innovation. It involves a critical analysis of your existing process and a willingness to shift from status quo.

Take a look at all of the steps that are involved in servicing a client. For example, buying a home involves a lender, a real estate agent, movers, escrow, title officers, home inspectors, and more. There are parts of this we can refer out and parts we can vertically integrate. In your sales or service process, are there vendors, suppliers, or service providers that would make sense to bring in-house? For example, if you currently outsource your marketing, it may be more effective and efficient to hire someone internally.

That said, be sure that you have maximized your effectiveness and efficiency with your core competencies before trying to take on new ones. You don't want to spread your resources too thin and become a jack of all trades who is a master of none. Laser focus and ever increasing expertise will help elevate you and your business faster.

You must ask yourself, "Have I maximized the quality of my client's experience and satisfaction with my core services?" If not, you have to start there. Remember to look for ways to reinforce your value proposition throughout your clients' interaction with you and your sales process. Can you go paperless for certain steps? Can you create "Wow" moments for your clients to remember? What can you do that will make the client say, "Wow, I didn't expect that, but it was great!"

As an example, there is an agent in our network who sends his clients to the movies or lunch while he conducts open houses at their property. They have to be out of the house anyway, and this gives them something fun to do. This gift is a small, but effective, "wow" moment. It also gives his clients a story to tell their friends, which ultimately leads to referral business.

Anticipation means staying ahead of your client's wants by providing them with conveniences before it occurs to them to ask.

3. Position yourself as a media resource.

Remember, social proof and third party validation are two of the best forms of marketing you can get. When you say something about yourself, people believe about half of what you say. When someone else says the same thing about you, more people tend to listen and believe it all. Thus peer-to-peer review websites have grown in popularity. When people don't feel tied to a company or service, they usually give a less biased review.

Being quoted as an expert by the media positions you as a trusted resource. Look for ways to get in front of your target audience through media channels. Comment on blogs. Offer market stats and information to reporters. When media outlets turn to you as an expert, you are on the fast track to incoming leads.

I was surprised to hear from my media contacts that they often struggle to find sources for quotes and that many agents didn't return their calls. I have continued to make myself available to media contacts, and it has helped my marketing and credibility tremendously. The reporters and writers know they can come to me and rely on me to follow up promptly.

Writing articles and blogs about what is going on in your industry is also a great way to position yourself as an industry expert. Most people under-utilize media to build their personal brand. Write about trends in your industry or even trends in a related industry. For example, many luxury home buyers also like luxury automobiles. An article about the newest Lamborghini may be just as interesting as one about an amazing home.

These days, you can even use social media, such as Facebook, Twitter, Instagram, and LinkedIn. The key with social media is to share and be informative about your industry while maintaining a personal touch. Include a good balance of your personal interests and personality in your posts to keep them from coming across as too "salesy." Also, be sure to create posts that support your passion for the sports and entertainment niche. Try to be genuine without alienating people. You can root for your team without talking too much trash about the other team. You may end up with a client from your rival team, and you would hate to get fired for having burned their jersey on social media.

People will often repost your article or information, giving you an even bigger audience. Some industries have regulations on how you can advertise, so make sure you comply with any and all applicable rules.

I once wrote an article entitled, "10 Best Practices When Working With Celebrity Clients." It was featured on Zillow and helped reinforce my position in this niche as an expert. Other media outlets saw this article and also reached out to me for quotes. I also reposted the article on my social media channels. Most importantly, I picked up a couple of clients from it.

4. Fail Fast, Fail Forward

Fail fast and move on. If you have given a new product, service, marketing campaign, or new business strategy an ample trial period and it is not working, don't be afraid to shift gears and try something new. It can be tricky knowing when to abandon a strategy. Therefore, it's important to track your efforts and measure your outcomes. It's is the only way to gauge the results. You may ultimately find that you only need to make a minor adjustment to an existing strategy versus changing it altogether.

When you "fail," take the opportunity to learn from the mistakes, so that you can move your business forward. Trying to make everything perfect before implementation can be a roadblock to moving forward. Here is one of my favorite examples that supports this theory:

[Note: This excerpt is from Fail Fast, Fail Often: How Losing Can Help You Win *by Ryan Babineaux, P.hD., and John Krumboltz, Ph.D., with the permission of Tarcher/ Penguin. Copyright 2013 Ryan Babineaux, Ph.D., and John Krumboltz, Ph.D.]*

In the book, *Art and Fear,* the artists Ted Orland and David Waylon share a story about a ceramics teacher who tried an experiment with his class.

The teacher divided the students into two groups. Those sitting on the left side of the studio were to be graded solely on the quantity of their work, while those on the right, solely on the quality. The instructor informed the students in the quantity group that a simple rule would be applied to evaluate their grades: those who produced fifty pounds of pots would get an A, those who produced forty pounds a B, and so on.

For the quality group, the instructor told the students that he would assign a course grade based on the single best piece produced over the duration of the course. So if a student created a first-rate pot on day one of the course and did nothing else for the term, he would still get an A.

When the end of the quarter arrived, and it came to grading time, the instructor made an interesting discovery: the students who created the best work, as judged by technical and artistic sophistication, were the quantity group. While they were busy producing pot after pot, they were experimenting, becoming more adept at working with the clay, and learning from the mistakes on each progressive piece.

In contrast, the students in the quality group carefully planned out each pot and tried to produce refined, flawless work, and so they only worked on a few pieces over the length of the course. Because of their limited practice, they showed little improvement.

5. Bundle Your Benefits

Your sports and entertainment clients should know that you or your firm is the only place to get the specific services that fit their needs.

Only you, your team, or your company should be able to offer the unique set of benefits that you advertise to clients. These benefits should be well defined, easily articulated, always delivered, and impossible for your competition to duplicate.

You may offer several individual products or services that your competition also offers. Which of these products or services can be bundled together so that you can save your clients time and money? By offering them more, you are delivering identifiable value over your competition. Again, remember that you must deliver high level, expert service for anything you are offering.

Adding on or bundling services may be something you do after you are well established in your core competency. You are best served by having an established reputation for delivering on your core product or service; then it is easier to offer your client base the additional services.

6. Be Tech Savvy

Technology is one of the best ways to stay ahead of your competition. Most athletes and entertainers have been exposed to and are accustomed to using the latest technology and gadgets. What new technology is available for your industry? What technology originally developed for another industry can you use in yours?

> **Only you, your team, or your company should be able to offer the unique set of benefits that you advertise to clients. These benefits should be well defined, easily articulated, always delivered, and impossible for your competition to duplicate.**

Even if your industry is not technology driven, are there elements of technology that can be utilized to improve your process and how you service your clients? Can you separate yourself or your company from your competition by using technology?

Make sure that the technology you decide to implement is not too advanced for your clients to use. Also, make sure it is not too advanced for you! While most athletes and entertainers tend to be tech savvy, some technology has a learning curve that is too great for quick implementation. Technology changes constantly, but you should not force clients to change at the same pace. It is okay to have frequent internal changes that improve your processes, but the interface with your clients should only change when absolutely necessary or enormously beneficial.

7. Forget Me Not

"Forget me not," is the message you want to convey to all of your past clients. Mindshare is important for referrals and repeat business. Most satisfied consumers who don't refer or hire for repeat business would have done so if the sales associate had just kept in touch. When a new need arises, people often go with what's most convenient. If you can maintain that relationship, clients will take the extra step to seek you out again and go with the convenience of your tried and true service.

Acquiring clients is no easy task. It's way easier to keep a happy client than to find a new one. Once you have gone through the effort and expense to acquire a client, you should do everything you can to keep them as a client and get referral business.

Most of us are good at immediate follow-up, but not ongoing communication. We complete a transaction with a follow-up email or closing gift, but this isn't enough to stay top of mind down the road. Even if your product or service is a one and done type, you can still benefit from word of mouth and referral business. Athletes especially look to their teammates for referrals. Be sure your name is on the tip of their tongue.

Stay in touch with them. Do lunches, golf, or other sporting events. It is easier to get people to commit to something casual and fun, versus yet another work event.

Treat business managers and agents as well as you treat your clients. These gatekeepers can be ongoing sources of business.

Don't bombard your sports and entertainment clients or their representatives with unnecessary emails, calls, or information. Their time is limited and valuable, just like yours. Only reach out with valuable information or updates you're sure they'll appreciate. Quarterly touches are generally enough for your database of sports and entertainment contacts to keep you top of mind. Obviously, reach out more often if your business requires it. Lead with useful information or services, not just updates on your accomplishments or how great you are.

Technology changes constantly, but you should not force clients to change at the same pace.

FOCUS & FINISH TIP:

Find ways to stay in front of your clients and earn mindshare. When they think of your industry, they should think of you.

Next Steps

If you are like me, your mind is racing at this point. In a good way! You have most likely started writing your road map to a successful sports and entertainment based practice. Don't start too quickly. I have always liked the saying that marathon runners "Run slow to run fast." The saying came about because experienced runners usually run the second half of a marathon faster than the first. For our purposes, you should plan slowly for a more efficient and effective launch or expansion. Consider the following steps:

- Reread this book
    - I made this book short and to the point for a reason. As you know by now, my philosophy is Focus & Finish. It is a focus and finish book. Read it, reread it, and start to implement the strategies and game plan. I focused on the most important things to know and do to get you into action and production in this niche as quickly as possible.
- Write out your game plan (If it's not on a list, it doesn't exist).
    - Are you launching on your own or as a division within a firm?

    - Prioritize your plan
    - Create your collateral
    - Break it into manageable chunks
- Execute
    - Analyze the opportunity in your market for a sports and entertainment practice.
    - Identify your unique sales proposition.
    - Package and tailor your offering to athletes and entertainers.
    - Start your outreach program to go after business.
    - Analyze and modify as necessary.
- Continue to work on your business, not just in it.
- Focus & Finish

For additional tools, ongoing support, and sports and entertainment business opportunities, visit our SellebrityNetwork.com website.

About the Author

Kofi N. Nartey developed his expertise in the sports and entertainment aspects of real estate for over a decade. He is currently the National Director of the Compass Sports & Entertainment Division; a division he created and launched. Also a Certified Luxury Homes Marketing Specialist, Kofi joined Compass after successfully creating and managing the sports and entertainment division for his previous firm, The Agency. He was managing director for two other offices and managed the luxury homes division for another firm before that. His current sports and entertainment division consistently manages over $1 billion dollars in luxury real estate nationwide.

He attended and played football at the University of California at Berkeley and later completed his MBA in the Presidential and Key Executive Program at Pepperdine University. He also frequents the other side of the podium as a guest speaker and trainer for the *Institute for Luxury Home Marketing* and *Leaders in Luxury*, and has conducted trainings for almost every major real estate brand in North America. Kofi has also been a speaker for Inman Luxury Connect and the national Inman conference in San Francisco. Kofi has always looked to elevate the standard for real estate professionals by acting as a professional business consultant and not just an agent. He has been recognized and awarded for his negotiating, marketing, and sales abilities.

Kofi reached a professional level in sports and successfully worked as an actor for over ten years. He brings his vast industry contacts and experience to his business. His understanding of the sports and entertainment niche has enabled him to effectively service professional athletes, entertainers, and distinguished clientele since 2003, comprising over 100 sports and entertainment clients, including Michael Jordan.

Kofi has been a correspondent on celebrity and luxury real estate for over 100 national television and print media outlets including the Wall Street Journal, LA Times, Chicago Tribune, CBS, CNBC, NBC Sports, Bloomberg, Fox Business News, ESPN, CNN Money, The Insider, and others. He was also a regularly featured agent on HGTV's Selling LA, has made numerous appearances on Million Dollar Listing, and is a celebrity and luxury real estate correspondent on Hollywood Today Live. His exposure to the national and international real estate markets has enabled him to effectively market and sell properties locally, nationally, and internationally.

In 2017, to better service the sports and entertainment industry, Kofi created The Sports & Entertainment Society. It is a network of agents and service providers who focus on this niche. It is also a hub for training and information on celebrity real estate and lifestyles.

Kofi believes in honesty, integrity, and fun in business. He is a natural motivator and business builder and often consults with businesses on marketing and growth strategies. He currently sits on the advisory boards of three different start-ups. Kofi lives in Playa Vista, CA (Silicon Beach) with his amazing wife Mimi and children, Liya and Lincoln.